# Men of
# HONOR
# Women of
# VIRTUE

# MEN OF HONOR, WOMEN OF VIRTUE

## Educators

*This book is an excellent primer for those interested in establishing faith-based rites of passage. In* Men of Honor, Women of Virtue, *Chuck Stecker draws upon his rich and varied experience as parent, military man, churchman, and scholar to both exhort and to instruct the reader as we reclaim our children for the kingdom and help them establish a mature, adult faith.*

—Dr. Bradley J. Widstrom
Chair, Department of Youth and Family Ministries, Denver Seminary

*This book is an excellent and practical roadmap for appropriately reaching this and future generations for Jesus Christ.*

—Dr. Gary Sallquist
Headmaster, Miami Valley Christian Academy

## Ministry Leaders

*I know of no one who communicates with greater clarity and passion the need to pass on faith to our children and the next generation.* Men of Honor, Women of Virtue *is the book that most parents have been waiting for and church leaders should put this at the top of their reading list. Men of Honor and Women of Virtue does not just inform but it truly empowers parents and leaders to make a difference in the lives of their own sons and daughters.*

—Dr. Dave Wardell
Co-Founder, Promise Keepers

*Be alarmed; be very alarmed! What is happening within our churches, in our families, and beneath our noses is a multigenerational catastrophe. We are hemorrhaging our youth, and we are under an illusion that "they'll be back." Chuck Stecker has a powerful message that calls for our collective attention, prayers, and action.*

—Larry Malone
Director, United Methodist Men's Ministries

*In a time when we are seeing over 90 percent of the children of Christian families walk away from their parents' church and faith after high school, Chuck Stecker gives parents and ministry leaders a clear look at the problem and some desperately needed help.*

—Dr. Cornell "Corkie" Haan
National Facilitator for Spiritual Unity, Mission America

*Dr. Chuck Stecker has done a wonderful job illustrating parents' God-given responsibility to teach their children the truth regarding sexual purity. Too often this role is dismissed while the morality of our children continues to decline. Chuck points us back in the right direction—to God's calling for parents and children.*

—**Rick Schatz**
President, National Coalition for Protection of Children & Families

*For many years Chuck and I have talked about this book and his dream to equip people in their journey of faith. I, for one, am eager to get this book into the hands of many people who will be blessed and encouraged.*

—**Rod Handley**
President, Character That Counts

*If we are to have any chance of reproducing ourselves into our sons and daughters and have any confidence that they will in turn do the same, we will all need a double portion of Chuck Stecker's passion, wisdom, and firsthand experience. Follow him through these pages as he demonstrates how to run hard and, at the end of our own generational lap, to pass with care.*

—**R. Michael Tesdahl**
Col. USA, Ret. Officers' Christian Fellowship (OCF)
Director for Strategic Coordination and Volunteer Support

*Chuck Stecker is dangerous. Undeniably, enthusiastically, unalterably, unswervingly, steadfastly pursuant in his wild heart for God! And, he is intent on pulling you into the swirling storm of God's primitive power with him! Don't just read this book—experience it … let it grab you … the world needs more dangerous people like Chuck.*

—**Paul Louis Cole**
Christian Men's Network

*Finally someone who tells it like it really is! This book is timely, relevant, and biblical.*

—**Dr. A. D. Beacham, Jr.**
Executive Director of Missions,
International Pentecostal Holiness Church

*Chuck Stecker is the "real deal"—a man with an equally fiery passion for knowing God and for seeing young men and women commit themselves passionately to Jesus Christ. God has used him—and his powerful rites of passage—to help transform the lives of thousands of youth in America. I thank God that two were my twin daughters—way back in 1990.*

—**Dr. Bob Hamrin**
President, Great Dads

*Chuck Stecker has poured out his heart and given men a much needed manual. I urge men to read this book....put into action the principles and leave a godly legacy. That is our calling.*

—Jack Kelley
International Men's Ministry Director,
International Pentecostal Holiness Church

## Parents

*This book and Chuck's ministry teach churches how to enable young people to be a strategic part of our spiritual armed forces...in a war where there is no such thing as an "acceptable rate of loss."*

—Don and Shelly Larson, Denver, CO

*In Men of Honor, Women of Virtue, Chuck provides powerful concepts to deal with the issue of losing generations of young people in our churches. This book is a must read for parents and the church body.*

—Tom Morrison, Highlands Ranch, CO

*Men of Honor, Women of Virtue provides both individual and church families a Christ-based blueprint for developing, encouraging, and supporting our young men and women to attain their eternal, godly legacy. All parents should read this book!*

—Robert and Brenda Grizzle, Highlands Ranch, CO

## Pastors

*Serving as Chuck's pastor has placed me in the unique position to see him and his family in action. I can say very plainly that the passion and principles of this book are lived out daily in Chuck's life! Through Chuck's coaching and leadership, we are becoming a truly intergenerational church for God's glory! I am honored to highly recommend this text and this man as gifts for God's kingdom work.*

—Jim Ladd
Senior Pastor, Grace Community Church, Centennial, CO

*America is befuddled about how to navigate the journey from childhood to adulthood, and it's showing every day from the classroom to the boardroom. Sadly, when the church should be charting the course, it seems we've also lost our compass. Chuck Stecker's no-nonsense prophetic voice gives not only clarity but practical solutions for parents and Christian leaders who want to clear the path for our young people to follow Christ into maturity.*

—Bill Peel
Associate Pastor, Fellowship Bible Church, Dallas, TX

*Armed with a passion for Christ, a love for God's church, and intense desire to impact the youth of our culture with the glorious message of God, Chuck Stecker has nailed an urgent message for today and presented an antidote to the alarming statistics of the exodus of youth from today's church culture.*

—Larry Biggers
Senior Pastor, Northside Chapel, Columbus, GA

*Dr. Stecker's God-given insight in this book is like a lighthouse leading a searching generation to safe passage into adulthood.*

—M. Joseph Dugas
Senior Pastor, Crossroads Ministry Centre, Tioga, LA

*Chuck Stecker delivers a powerful and challenging message to the church. It's time to bridge the generations and stop the church's hemorrhaging by weaving the hearts of the younger generation into the fabric of the congregation as a whole. Expect to be stretched, challenged, and motivated by this positive, life-giving message.*

—Tim Woody
Senior Pastor, Caring First Assembly of God, Saint Joseph, MO

*Chuck Stecker is a prophetic voice to the church calling for intergenerational coopera-tion and coordination.* Men of Honor, Women of Virtue *is a must read for all seeking to understand what God is saying to the families of America at this hour. I highly recommend this book and A Chosen Generation ministry.*

—David A. Garcia
Lead Pastor, Brooksville Assembly of God, Brooksville, FL

*Chuck has an essential message to the church today. His seminar,* Men of Honor and Women of Virtue, *has had a huge and lasting impact on our church. I am thrilled to see this message in print for all to partake.*

—Doug Brown
Lead Pastor, Lee's Summit Community Church, Lee's Summit, MO

Men of Honor, Women of Virtue *changed our church. We went from a church that alienated our young adults to intentional and programmatically becoming a "cross-generational church." Our church has seen spiritual, relational, and numeri-cal growth both in families and especially in young adults.*

—Dr. Daniel L. Erickson
Associate Pastor, Lee's Summit Community Church, Lee's Summit, MO

*Chuck is powerful voice calling a generation of youth to rise up and be men and women of God. His teaching had a profound effect upon our young people, and that in turn eternally changed our church.*

—Gary Gray
Senior Pastor, Venice Assembly of God, Venice, FL

# MEN OF
# HONOR
## WOMEN OF
# VIRTUE

### THE POWER OF RITES OF PASSAGE
### INTO GODLY ADULTHOOD

# DR. CHUCK STECKER

**SEISMIC**
PUBLISHING GROUP

DENVER   NASHVILLE

Published by Seismic Publishing Group

http://seismicpg.com/

Second Printing, 2010
*Printed in the United States of America*

Originally published by David C. Cook Publishing, 2006, under the same title

The Web addresses (URLs) recommended throughout this book are solely offered as a resource to the reader. The citation of these Web sites does not in any way imply an endorsement on the part of the author or the publisher, nor does the author or publisher vouch for their content for the life of this book.

Cover Design By: Sofia Rossi
    sofia@firstlookdesignstudios.com

**Library of Congress Cataloging-in-Publication Data**
Stecker, Chuck, 1947-
    Men of honor, Women of virtue / Chuck Stecker.
        p. cm.
    Includes bibliographical references (p. ) and index.
ISBN 978-0-9843866-0-4 (alk. paper)
        1. Rites of passage—Christian. 2. Initiation rites—Religious aspects—
        Christianity. 3. Parenting teens—Christian. 4. Christian youth—Religious
        life. I. Title.

*To my mother, Shirlee Lee (1930–2003),*
*who taught me to dream—*
*"Hello, Love"*

*and*
*To my wife, Billie Jean,*
*who enables and pushes me to dream—*
*"Thank you, Love"*

# CONTENTS

## PART 1
## Where Are We and How Did We Get Here?

## PART 2

### Don't We Need to Know Where We're Going?

# PART 3

## Can Anyone Tell Me How to Get There?

# PART 4

## "Even Generations Yet to Be Born ..."

# FOREWORD

Our dream as Christian parents is for our children to keep walking with the Lord when they leave the nest. Chuck Stecker shows us that this is simply not happening. How can the number one desire we have for our children not come to pass?

We simply do not have a process in the Christian church that effectively engages our children to embrace their parents' faith as their own after leaving the nest. Often the spiritual well-being of our teens is delegated to a professional youth worker. Many observers now question the wisdom of culling our children out into a separated group. Chuck speaks eloquently about the age segregation of our youth from the adult population, which has become the norm.

Chuck and I first became friends a decade ago. We share a common passion for bridging the divide separating moms and dads from their sons and daughters. God called Chuck to take the extraordinary step of focusing his life on this single issue. Over the last ten years, I've watched him develop a powerful rite-of-passage experience. And the world will be a better place because he did.

It has always seemed curious to me that Christians do not already have a rite of passage for teenagers to graduate into manhood and womanhood. We need models for raising godly adult children. I think in this book you will see that Chuck has developed ideas for you and your children that could be lifesaving. He has fine-tuned a rite of passage that I wish had been around when I was a teenager.

This is simply a beautiful book—one man's thought-provoking journey to discover how the church can reverse the trend of losing our young adults to worldly ways. Chuck's thesis is that we are making Christian teenagers, but they are not becoming Christian adults. He's on to something here. This is a man who has been thinking deeply about how the church can raise up children who become adults who love, trust, and serve Jesus.

This is a passionate book, but not over the top. I found myself in tears several times and chuckling to myself frequently. The book teems with hope. It is rich in stories and common sense. His analogies are spot on. You'll find as he shares that he is a passionate yet level-headed thinker and writer.

But be aware: This book may rattle your cage and challenge your assumptions about teenagers. It offers a fresh and completely unique look at how to raise godly children.

Some people, of course, don't think teenagers have much substance, but I'm pretty sure those people must not know any teenagers. All the young people I've met want to do something with their lives, leave the world a better place, and learn what it means to be a man or a woman.

In my own work with teenage young men, I found they were deeply interested in how to be men. They wanted to know how to make wise decisions, how to get along with their families, how to find meaning and purpose, what their guidelines for dating should be, and why there is suffering. Perhaps more than anything, they just wanted to know someone cared.

In their late teens and twenties our children will make many of the most important decisions they will ever make—decisions like where to go to college, what career to pursue, where to live, and whom to marry. Ironically, these decisions must be made at a time when they are often least prepared to make them. You hold in your hands a manual that can equip them to choose well.

Dr. Patrick Morley
Chairman and CEO, Man in the Mirror
Winter Park, Florida

# ACKNOWLEDGMENTS

My life and this book have been shaped by many people. It is hard for me to imagine any author arriving at the moment of publishing his first book (and now going into a second printing) and honestly stating that he has done so on his own. The pages of this book contain the thoughts and dreams of many people in my life.

## Special Thanks to

Frank and Dee Maycock, for investing your lives in me and; as the years went on, my entire family. Dee, you have been praying for me for over 45 years (and you are only 50 years young).

Dr. Orv Menard, for guiding my first major writing effort and for suggesting I write for publication. And perhaps most important, for introducing me to Cyrano.

Bill Peel, for your encouragement and guidance and for teaching me how to write a formal book proposal.

Troy Reichert, personal friend and board member of A Chosen Generation (ACG), for capturing the vision for publishing this book and for bringing me to Orlando at your expense to meet with prospective publishers.

I am still very grateful to the David C. Cook publishing team for first printing of Men of Honor Women of Virtue.

The Executive Team of *The Seismic Group* is an incredible group of men. In no particular order, Bob Grizzle, Ken Larson, Ray Morgan and Troy Reichert have been the greatest group of men to work with on this project that any author could want. Together we are believing to be a part of a world-wide movement to restore the "InterGenerational" church and family.

Frank Burrows, for introducing me to the concept of the "family blessing" and for always loving me enough to tell me what I needed to hear.

Gary Sallquist, for never wavering as my friend and brother for nearly forty years and Joyce for being always the encourager and for "chocolate-covered" strawberries.

"Children of Light," for teaching me more than I could have taught them.

For Neil Markva, teacher extraordinaire of Biblical truth.

My colleagues at Promise Keepers—Dr. Rick Kingham, who hired me, Dan Schaffer, Chuck Lane, Dave Wardell, Gordon England and Bill McCartney—for investing in me and being my friends and encouragers.

James Ryle, for spoon-feeding me on the concepts of "Rites of Passage."

Promise Keepers regional directors and staff—Chad, Doc, Wendell, Dan, Alvin, Gary R, Andy, Louis, Kerry, Paul, Carl, Gary S, Mark, Diane, Beth, Charlie, Bill, George, Ogie, Marla, Johnny and many others—for making an indelible mark on the way I view ministry. What a run we had together. You will never know how many lives God touched through you and your selfless sacrifices.

The men of the National Coalition of Men's Ministries, for being some of the greatest supporters for me and this book. You guys are terrific.

Dan Schaffer, who processed many of the concepts with me, including the "father's blessing," and who loves me too much to let me get by with anything shabby for God regardless of what it looks like to others.

Brenda Snailum, former vice president of ACG, and faculty member, for spending many long hours helping to shape the thoughts and message of the ministry in the early days.

Ray Morgan, my friend, brother, travel partner and "armor bearer" since 1998, not only for serving on the board of trustees for ACG, but also for his unwavering support and encouragement. Mary Morgan, for being Ray's wife and my sister.

Becky Lichtenwalter, ACG Executive Assistant and ministry prayer coordinator, for taking a significant load from my desk, allowing me to meet my writing deadlines. You never let me leave home without prayer coverage.

Pastor Joseph (Maurice) Dugas and the other visionary pastors from nearly seventy churches, for trusting ACG to conduct rites of passage in their congregations.

Jim Ladd, senior pastor of my church, for not only encouraging us and being a champion for Rites of Passage and intergenerational ministry, but also for understanding what it means to be a "pastor."

Andy Sloan, for outstanding editing of the intial manuscript and for owning the work with me, and for providing insights and thoughts that significantly helped me personally.

Pat Morley, who is quick to tell everyone that "a rising tide raises the level of all boats," meaning that what is good for the church or ministry is good for everyone. Pat does not just believe in ministries but works very hard to help them. I am blessed and grateful for his investing in me and this book and writing the foreword.

Billie, my wife, for being my encourager, friend, sounding board, and greatest ally in this project and others throughout the years. Billie has been willing to sacrifice anything and everything for God to have his way. This book wouldn't have been completed without her.

Our children, their spouses and our grandchildren, who cheered on the book at every point and sacrificed family time to allow me to write. At one point, our granddaughter Hannah, then five years old, asked, "Papa, is that book done yet?" She was letting me know that she and Eliana had given up some time with me and Grandma and that was fine but we needed to get moving and finish!

To the many readers who grabbed every copy of the first printing, I am very grateful for your encouragement and your support. Your words to me personally have been a source of incredible encouragement.

The many supporters of ACG. Your trust in this ministry means more than I can express except to say thank you, and may God truly bless you.

To Almighty God be the glory.

# INTRODUCTION

As a teenager, I bought the lie all those '60s movies communicated: that downing a six-pack of beer, having sex in the backseat of a car, and bragging about it to your friends would make you a man. It didn't work—not for me or for anyone else I knew.

I couldn't allow my sons to follow that path. Although I didn't have a strategy or any experience to guide me, I was convinced God had a better plan for them. One thing I knew for sure: I didn't want my sons to carry a hole in their hearts for as long as I had. That commitment started me on an incredible journey. I wasn't looking to start a ministry, earn a Doctor of Ministry degree, or take on the world's upside-down value system. I was just trying to be a good dad and give my sons the best possible understanding of manhood. I didn't merely want to hope they turned out well. I wanted to launch them with an understanding—from God's perspective—of what it means to be a man.

Though I told people I'd someday write a book about my daughter and two sons, and even picked a title—*What a Heavenly Father Can Do in Spite of an Earthly Father*—I missed the season of launching my daughter into godly womanhood. Several reasons accounted for this. I didn't know who I was created to be, for one thing. I didn't clearly understand manhood, for another. As a result, it was virtually impossible for me to guide my daughter into godly womanhood. Fortunately, God had his hand on her; and in spite of her earthly father, her heavenly Father helped her steer through some pretty rough waters. By the time my sons were approaching manhood, my daughter had already found her womanhood in the Lord. I say this to assure the reader that manhood for my sons was not more important to me than my daughter's womanhood.

In the beginning I was pretty clueless regarding rites of passage and God's plan for young men and women. Consequently, I sought materials and people that might clarify this issue. Without knowing what I was looking for, I trusted I'd know it when I found it.

In 1996, I discovered several books and articles on rites of passage. I learned that James Ryle, senior pastor of Boulder Valley Vineyard Christian Fellowship in Boulder, Colorado, and a member of the Board of Directors of Promise Keepers, had been conducting rites of passage for the young men in his church for several years. Pastor Ryle met with me and gave me the materials he had created. More-over, he spent several hours explaining the biblical concepts behind the ceremony he had developed and his dreams for his sons and the men in his church. He also shared his personal journey. We discovered a common childhood loss; both our dads had been in prison when we most needed their help navigating our way into manhood. Maybe because of this, we both felt a strong desire to help other men find their God-given manhood.

I ALSO SAW A REMARKABLE MOVE OF GOD WHEN THE PASTOR GAVE AN INVITATION FOR MEN WHO HAD NEVER RECEIVED THEIR FATHERS' "BLESSING" INTO GODLY MANHOOD TO COME FORWARD.

Later that year, I shared my burden for rites of passage with several fellow staff members of Promise Keepers. Within a few months, a great friend and brother, Paul Osborne, called to ask if I would conduct a rite-of-passage ceremony for a church in Knoxville, Tennessee. I accepted, and in January 1997, I stumbled through a weekend rite of passage that resulted in seven boys becoming young men, including my older son, Chad. My younger son, Courtney, witnessed the ceremony.

I also saw a remarkable move of God when the pastor gave an invitation for men who had never received their fathers' "blessing" into godly manhood to come forward. Nearly half the men assembled asked to be blessed and received into godly manhood.

In July 1997, I resigned from the staff of Promise Keepers to begin a new ministry. My vision was to minister to men in the military, work at leadership training, and develop rites of passage for churches. At that time, I believed rites of passage were to be the third priority.

The concept of *Men of Honor, Women of Virtue* came into being that summer when Truman Abbott, the administrator of Christian

Fellowship School in Denver, asked me to speak at their high school retreat. I firmly believe that God gives us "spiritual markers"; this retreat became one of those.

Having conducted only one rite of passage, I was by no means an authority on the subject. Still, the essential message of *Men of Honor, Women of Virtue* and the key points for each session were as coherent as anything I have ever presented. Truman and I agreed a full-blown rite of passage wasn't appropriate in this setting because the students' parents and pastors were not present. We concluded the retreat with a time of blessing that fulfilled the needs of young men and women hungry for older men and women to bless them and believe in them. I also saw the value of young men and women hearing the same messages and definitions together. Issues of purity and godly values provided them a foundation of truth and would become "anchor points" for both genders.

Toward the end of 1997, Pastor Maurice Dugas, senior pastor of Crossroads Ministry Centre in Tioga, Louisiana, asked me to conduct a rite of passage for his church. The big difference between this rite of passage and anything I had seen or done before was that this would be the first one to include the entire church. Until this time, all I had seen or been trained to do was a rite of passage for sons by their fathers. I had realized, though, that something was missing without the daughters, mothers, and the entire church family being present and involved in the ceremony.

> IT WASN'T JUST ABOUT THE YOUTH—GOD TOUCHED THE ENTIRE CONGREGATION WITH A NEW UNDERSTANDING OF GODLY ADULTHOOD.

I was not prepared for what I witnessed at the "Mighty Church on the Curve." It wasn't just about the youth—God touched the entire congregation with a new understanding of godly adulthood.

Up to this point, my main ministry had been to men. In addition, having served for nearly twenty-three years in the military, I understood the concept of retention rates and what it took to keep good soldiers. But I'd never thought to apply that knowledge to the church at large. I didn't realize how many young men and women were drifting from church. The congregations our family had been involved with had strong ministries, so we hadn't yet experienced the "Bermuda Triangle" into which young men and women seemed to disappear.

Over the next few years, my eyes were opened and my priorities inverted. Ministry to men in the military and leadership training took a backseat to trying to meet the church's crying need to reach and keep our own children. It became quite apparent that the primary, though unspoken, issue was not evangelism but stewardship. The church is trying to reach the world while losing its own children.

**THE CHURCH IS TRYING TO REACH THE WORLD WHILE LOSING ITS OWN CHILDREN.**

Since that small beginning, our message of passage into godly adulthood has traveled to more than forty states and several foreign countries. The issue, while terribly significant, does not appear to be complicated. Churches—and families—have abdicated their responsibilities to define, affirm, recognize, and confirm godly manhood and womanhood for our sons and daughters. We have rolled over and let the culture of the world define adulthood for our children. Whether through movies, sex, drinking, driving, or any other activity that allegedly marks adulthood, we have let others tell our children what it means to be a man or woman.

Parents and churches are not doing their part. Therefore, another generation is being lost. A sense of clarity regarding adulthood has slipped away from us. Several generations ago it may have seemed obvious when a boy became a man or a girl became a woman. Unfortunately, adulthood wasn't spiritually founded; instead, it was based on when a child could work and share the load. Unlike cultures that truly celebrate the passage into adulthood, our Western civilization takes it for granted. We essentially let the concept of adulthood slip away by buying into a concept of adolescence that allows our children to quit being kids while not becoming adults.

Much of the problem today may stem from the fact that our parents were never blessed into adulthood. It just seemed to happen for them, and as a result they weren't sure of what to do for their own children. My dad never received from his dad a blessing or any spiritual markers in his own life. Therefore, he wasn't able to help me enter into adulthood. My father couldn't pass on or give what he didn't have.

Perhaps your parents came from similar circumstances. They may not have given you the help you needed. Unjustified expectations can lead to resentment. If that's the case for you, I pray this book will empower you to forgive your parents for not giving you what you needed.

## What Is Adulthood?

Before we examine the topic of adulthood, we must first define the term. When you hear that word, several words immediately come to mind: *maturity, responsibility,* and *independence,* to name a few. These are good starting points, but there's more to being an adult than being a certain age, being on time, and doing your own laundry.

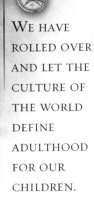

WE HAVE ROLLED OVER AND LET THE CULTURE OF THE WORLD DEFINE ADULTHOOD FOR OUR CHILDREN.

In discussing the subject of adulthood with many people, I've observed that we tend to set our perceived requirements for younger generations much higher than for our own or older age groups. We can look at people our own age or older and, regardless of how incredibly immature they may act, still regard them as adults simply because of the year they were born. Yet teenagers must meet an unspecified performance level to be considered adults. Then, should they do something we regard as immature, we quickly point out that they are not really adults and put them again in a position of earning their adulthood from us.

A second controversial issue surrounding the topic of adulthood pertains to denominational differences, or what I refer to as "faith distinctives." The concepts of this book are not based on a person's church affiliation. God's plan for adulthood should simply be God's plan, regardless of where a person chooses to worship. Many of the battles in the body of Christ are not over truth but rather are a result of placing a higher value on our personal preferences and political beliefs than on the truth of God. In the same letter in which the apostle Paul affirmed that "all Scripture is God-breathed," he charged

Timothy: "Do your best to present yourself to God as one approved, a workman who does not need to be ashamed and who correctly handles the word of truth. Avoid godless chatter, because those who indulge in it will become more and more ungodly" (2 Tim. 2:15–16).

Whether I speak in a Methodist, Presbyterian, Assembly of God, Baptist, Vineyard, Covenant, Episcopal, or nondenominational church, the principles I teach remain the same. At the conclusion of a rite-of-passage ceremony in his church, one pastor told me, "There is not one thing you have taught or shared about that I now have to reteach, clarify, or undo. We don't even get that from speakers within our own denomination!"

PARENTS, NO MATTER THE AGES OF YOUR CHILDREN, IT IS NOT TOO LATE. I BELIEVED FOR MANY YEARS THAT BECAUSE OF MY OWN FAILURES AND MISSED OPPORTUNITIES, I HAD LOST THE CHANCE TO CHANGE SOME THINGS FOR MY OWN KIDS. NOT TRUE.

And, of course, there are great differences between men and women, yet the foundations for both are the same. Responsibility, salvation, trust, purity, and self-control are not specific male or female issues. Granted, how we are taught to apply them in our lives may be gender specific, but godly character is required of us all.

Finally, my heart's desire is to contribute to the strategies and resources needed for intentional inter-generational relationships and ministry. If the church is truly a family, every generation is needed and has value.

This book is far from being the final answer on the concepts of rites of passage. Perhaps the greatest contribution of this effort may be to energize parents and the church to reach and keep this generation in the belief that they can accomplish far more than we have for the glory of God.

For many years I have heard parents say, "I want my kids to have it better than I did." In virtually every case, they referred to material comforts. While there's nothing wrong with that sentiment, most of us want so much more for our kids than just a nice car or a comfortable house. We know our kids will face struggles and pain regardless of their economic status, so we must help them become more mature spiritually and lay a solid foundation of truth that will help them live above and beyond the circumstances they face as they grow.

Parents, no matter the ages of your children, it is not too late. I believed for many years that because of my own failures and missed opportunities, I had lost the chance to change some things for my own kids. Not true. We must stay in the battle for the lives and souls of our children, which includes our "adult" children. As our children grow, our techniques may change, but our goals remain the same or become even better focused. I don't know of a "perfect family." (Unfortunately, many Christian books do more to remind me of my imperfections than to provide logical and workable methods to help me improve.) We are all less than perfect and have less-than-perfect families; my prayer is that this book will help imperfect families who are trying to do "just a little better."

I believe more than ever before that a path into adulthood, and the support to walk that path to spiritual maturity, is the greatest need our children have—and therefore the greatest responsibility we have as parents.

# READERS' GUIDE

The markers for adulthood have taken on many forms and changed drastically over the years. Families and churches are certainly at a crisis point. Each of us has arrived at the point of adulthood by traveling different paths. The purpose of this guide is to help us, as parents and "spiritual parents," begin to truly understand where we are starting, where we want to go, and the best way to get there.

Watching our children walk in the fullness of their own faith is a joy. My hope is that this book will help adults of all ages understand their own journey—how they arrived at their current point in life and why certain issues have been so confusing.

The questions for each chapter will enable you to guide your children toward spiritual maturity. Four of the chapters (chapters 13–16) and the corresponding Readers' Guide activities are specifically intended for you to study and discuss with your children.

I encourage you to open your hearts as well as your minds. Some of the questions may be difficult, even painful. But if you persevere, you will reap great benefit. You can't take your children where you have not been or are not willing to go. So, be honest with God and yourself. If you study this book as part of a group, be honest with your group.

May God bless you in your efforts to faithfully lead and care for your family.

# PART

# 1

# WHERE ARE WE AND HOW DID WE GET HERE?

# YOU CAN'T GIVE
# WHAT YOU DON'T HAVE

I remember that weekend as if it took place only a few days ago. We were at a Christian retreat site in the mountains of eastern Tennessee. A church had gathered its men and sons and asked me to be a part of a rite of passage to help usher these young men into godly adulthood. This was the first rite of passage I had ever done. Although I have since come to believe that the rites of passage need to be conducted in the context of the entire church, this one was in an all-male environment.

Both of my sons accompanied me on this trip, and the older of the two would himself participate in this rite of passage into manhood. That alone would have been enough to chisel this weekend into my heart, but it wasn't the entire story.

I knew the mere sight of young men being blessed into godly adulthood might stir something in some of the older men who had never known that blessing in their own lives, so I spoke with the pastor ahead of time to prepare him for the possibilities. At the conclusion of the ceremonial rites of passage for seven young men, the pastor moved seamlessly into the next spiritual moment.

### The Father's Blessing

He invited any men who had never known their fathers' blessing before to receive that blessing as a son and a man. Without hesitation, nearly half the men stepped out of the room so they might be called in by name and received by the men of the church.

I immediately recognized the first man to step to the door. He was one of the fathers who had just called his own fifteen-year-old son out of childhood and into manhood. I had listened to him just a few minutes earlier struggle to get the words out. When he finally did, he began to weep. I thought at the time that he was overcome with emotion seeing his son being welcomed into manhood, but now I realized his tears had not been so much for his son as for himself. As he was calling his son into a season of life, he realized that he, as the father, had never known true godly manhood. I watched this man enter the room and walk between the two columns of the men of the church. He then knelt down before the pastors and elders of his church. It was in that moment I witnessed something I'm sure I will never forget.

> WITHOUT HESITATION, NEARLY HALF THE MEN STEPPED OUT OF THE ROOM SO THEY MIGHT BE CALLED IN BY NAME AND RECEIVED BY THE MEN OF THE CHURCH.

Before any of the pastors or elders could pray for him, another man stepped forward: His own fifteen-year-old son draped himself over his father's kneeling body on the floor. The opening words of his prayer still ring in my ears today: "My God, my God, you know how long I have waited for this moment!" From the mouth of his fifteen-year-old son came the truth. He had recognized the hole in his father's heart—the inadequacy his dad felt as a man. There before his very eyes he got to see the wounded heart of his father healed.

The following day we all came down from the mountain and attended church together. At the conclusion of the service a woman came directly toward me with tears in her eyes. These were not tears of pain; rather, there was a glow to her face. Without an introduction, she said, "I don't know what happened on that mountain this weekend, but I know this—I sent two boys to the mountains and God sent me back two men."

Now it registered. This was the wife of the man whose fifteen-year-old son had draped his body over his father's body to pray for him. She, indeed, had received back two men.

## A Neglected Necessity

In the eight years that have followed that initial rite of passage, I have watched pastors and elders, men and women, come to realize they had never known their fathers' blessing—and that, never having received that blessing, they had nothing to give. It was as if they were trying, in a spiritual sense, to write checks from a bank account that had been opened but in which a deposit had never been made.

Before you think that a person who's never known a father's blessing is a reflection of poor parenting, understand that for the most part, our parents have never known the blessing. It's been lost in our society, lost in our culture, and lost in our churches.

The words spoken to Jesus at his baptism—"This is my beloved Son, in whom I am well pleased" (Matt. 3:17 KJV)—have rarely been heard by today's generation of parents. How then, if we have never known our fathers' blessing, can we pass it on to another generation? We cannot give what we do not possess.

"I SENT TWO BOYS TO THE MOUNTAINS AND GOD SENT ME BACK TWO MEN."

## Testimonies of Healing

I've watched one pastor stand before his congregation and openly confess that he had never known a father's blessing. He said, "I've known a father's *blasting*, yes, but never a father's *blessing*." He went on to share that as a result of his realization, he had just spent the previous thirty minutes in the prayer room with the elders of his church, who had prayed over him as fathers would pray over their own sons. He said that now, for the first time, he was able to pray as a father and not just as their pastor.

In another church, as the pastor prepared to invite anyone who had never known a father's blessing to come forward, he paused, and for a few moments couldn't even continue. Then he said to his congregation, "I can't do this—because I have nothing to give you." Turning to me, he said that his own father was with the Lord; would I stand in as a spiritual father to pass on to him the blessing his father was never able to give? Within moments his wife was kneeling next to him, for she, too, had never known a father's blessing.

When the pastor and his wife rose to their feet that night, amid the tears of his congregation, he told his church family he thought he had received the blessing through ordination and other achievements, but he knew now that wasn't true. That night God had first revealed the hole in his heart and then healed the hurt.

I suggest that the failure on the part of our parents to pass on a blessing to us is primarily based upon the fact that they themselves never received a blessing.

## My Own Story

It was September 24, 1994. I had been on staff with Promise Keepers as the new Regional Director for the South Central Region of the United States for a little more than three weeks. While in Knoxville, Tennessee, I heard of an event called "When Men Pray," led by Pastor Onnie Kirk, and decided to drive to Nashville. I found myself, that Saturday morning, at the Ryman Auditorium—better known as the Grand Ole Opry—with a group of more than four hundred men who had gathered to pray.

I SUGGEST THAT THE FAILURE ON THE PART OF OUR PARENTS TO PASS ON A BLESSING TO US IS PRIMARILY BASED UPON THE FACT THAT THEY THEMSELVES NEVER RECEIVED A BLESSING.

In the middle of our prayers, Pastor Kirk interrupted the gathering by saying, "There are men here who have never known their fathers' blessing." He went on to explain that as a result of having never known our fathers' blessing, many of us were still seeking to earn or prove ourselves worthy of our earthly father's love—even though nothing could be further from God's plan. My eyes were suddenly opened to a new revelation. I had considered my heavenly Father's love and my earthly father's love as almost one and the same. If my earthly father did not love and bless me unconditionally, how could my heavenly Father? Pastor Kirk told us God loved us unconditionally, but many of us had never received that love. He gave a challenge: "If you are one of the men here who have never known the father's blessing, stand to your feet."

A rush of emotions came over me, and I knew immediately what had been missing in my life for so many years. I had spent my entire life trying to earn my earthly father's love so I could feel worthy, and without realizing it, I was also trying to earn my heavenly Father's love. Although I wasn't the only one in the room to stand that morning, it wouldn't have mattered if I had been. As I stood, the Reverend Don Finto and several other men gathered around me. Don took me in his arms and prayed a father's blessing over me as if I were his only son. I was released! I had nothing else to prove! My heavenly Father's love was unconditional—I couldn't do anything that would make him love me more, and I couldn't do anything that would make him love me less. For the first time, I felt I was, in fact, worthy to be called God's valuable son.

> HE COULD NOT GIVE WHAT HE DID NOT POSSESS, AND IT WASN'T HIS FAULT.

In the months following my experience in Nashville, I located my dad in Wichita, Kansas, after a separation of twelve years. Within the few short years that followed our reunion, God opened the door for me to share with my own dad about God our Father and his Son who died on a cross that we might be free.

One month short of my father's seventieth birthday, we knelt together in that small apartment in Wichita, where he asked Jesus Christ to be his Lord and Savior. Through that time together, God also revealed to me that my dad had never known a father's blessing. My father had been adopted, and I can honestly say that until that day in Wichita, he had lived with a birth certificate on which the word "unknown" was printed in the place where a father's name would have been typed. On that day in March 1997, my dad realized he had a real Father who loved him unconditionally. My father was unable to pass on a blessing to me or my brothers or sisters because he himself had never known that blessing. He could not give what he did not possess, and it wasn't his fault.

## It's Not Too Late

The lack of blessing on the part of fathers is not limited only to their sons; many daughters as well have never known their fathers' blessing. And the elements of the blessing are no different whether you are giving it or receiving it. But the spiritual implications are very simple: You cannot give what you do not possess.

I have come to believe that so much of our performance-driven lives is based on our need to be received unconditionally and blessed for who we are, not for what we do. In regard to growing our children in their faith, it's been said that the acorn doesn't fall far from the tree. If we parents cling tightly to the hurt in our own hearts due to the lack of a father's blessing, it's hard to imagine how we can help our children walk in the fullness of who God created them to be.

If you're wondering where you are when it comes to the issue of your father's blessing, ask yourself the following questions: Can you remember the day you got your driver's license? Can you remember the day you graduated from high school? Can you remember the days you succeeded or failed at anything in life? Can you also remember the day your father took you in his arms, held you tightly, and proclaimed for you to know in heaven and on earth that you were his beloved son or daughter and that he blessed you unconditionally with a father's love because of who you are and not for what you had done or even failed to do?

If you remember that day, you have something to give. If you can't remember that day, you can do something about it.

## Take the Initiative

The first step for me was to release my dad. Notice I didn't say "forgive" him. My dad hadn't done anything that required me to forgive him. I had held him responsible for my desire to please him; that was my need—not his fault. This may sound really strange to you, but after not seeing my dad for more than twelve years, I asked him to forgive me for the bitterness and anger I felt toward him. As a son, I am required by God to honor my father and mother.

The second step was actually receiving the blessing. Pastor Onnie Kirk opened the door for me. If your father is still living and you can go directly to him for a blessing, I suggest you do so.

Some might think that those who've never known the father's blessing were probably raised in a non-Christian home. In *The Prayer of Jabez Devotional,* Bruce Wilkinson told the story of his own son asking for his blessing:

> I remember the evening my son David asked me for a blessing.... "Dad, I want to ask you a question. Will you bless me?"
>
> His mom and sister stared at him. I stared at him as well, as his request appeared to drop out of the blue. "David, you know I do bless you," I said. "No, Dad. I want you to really bless me." Then he stood up, walked to the armchair where I was seated, and knelt in front of me. Then he waited, head bowed, without even looking up.
>
> Do you know what flooded through my heart at that moment? I felt a tremendous desire to bestow on him every possible good thing. Here was my own child waiting at my feet, telling me by word and action what he wanted most was what only I, his father, could give him....
>
> In Jesus' name, I poured blessing after blessing upon him. And I didn't stop until I was certain that he not only was blessed, but that he also felt blessed![1]

When asked by their children to bless them, I have seen fathers respond with the most incredible love and prayer of blessings. I watched a man in his late forties ask his parents, who were in their seventies, for their blessing. They were completely overcome with emotion and poured out blessings on their son.

In the event that your father is unavailable, God the Father is raising up spiritual fathers and mothers. Perhaps you could ask those who have been your "spiritual parents" to pray a blessing over you. Ideally, approach your pastor and ask him to bless you. Through no fault of their own, some pastors may not completely understand this concept. Remember that many have never received the blessing themselves. If your pastor needs some assistance, there are some very good resources that can help him. *The Blessing,* by Gary Smalley and John Trent, is the foundational source. I also recommend a wonderful book by Rolf Garborg titled *The Family Blessing.* Additional resources are listed in the back of this book.

This chapter has been difficult for some of you to read. I wish it could have been easier. If it was painful for you, remember this: We must find the source of our pain before the healing can begin.

I encourage you to ask yourself this question: What do I want to pass on to my children—wounds or health?

## FOR PERSONAL REFLECTION OR GROUP DISCUSSION

1. Describe the day you received your driver's license.

2. Describe your high school graduation.

3. Describe the event that would most closely resemble a father's blessing in your life.

4. Have you received a blessing from a "spiritual father"? Describe the person and the circumstances.

5. If your own parents have not blessed you, can you release them without hurt and anger?

6. If you have never known that blessing, whom do you have in your life to stand in as a spiritual father to bless you? How and when will you ask that person?

## CHAPTER 2

# "HOUSTON, WE HAVE A PROBLEM"

Upon my arrival at a Denver-area church on February 1, 2003, I was asked if I had heard the news. The *Columbia* space shuttle had apparently disappeared somewhere over Texas within minutes of its anticipated landing back at the Kennedy Space Center. As time went on, others arriving at the church continued to report the news indicating that the *Columbia* was lost, but no one had additional information or specific details. Shortly before we began breakfast, the fears of all the men present were confirmed. Somewhere over Texas, the *Columbia* space shuttle had literally disintegrated in midair, and all seven crew members were lost.

It didn't take very long for the reports to start coming in that across the Western states, even as far as California, there had been indications in the sky that something abnormal was happening. Far too late for anyone to do anything about it, the signs only proved to be precursors of an impending tragedy.

Within the days and weeks that followed, e-mails poured in from various sources indicating that the problem could have been foreseen. Apparently, a liftoff problem had not only been seen, but videotaped. One person went so far as saying the disaster of the *Columbia* space shuttle was set in motion at takeoff. Following the launch, there was virtually nothing that could have been done to stop the disaster.

As so often happens after an incident of this nature, many question whether the cost of life is really worth what we are gaining through space exploration. They would be quick to point out the other space shuttle tragedies. Many of us would think back to seventeen years ago when the *Challenger* exploded less than a minute after liftoff. All seven crew members were killed, including Christa McAuliffe, the first teacher to be in space. And while generally not mentioned in many news stories, some of us still remember January 27, 1967, the day a fire on the launchpad engulfed *Apollo 1*, killing all three astronauts— Virgil Grissom, Roger Chaffee, and Edward White.

Here were three tragedies at three different stages of their missions. *Apollo 1* never lifted off the ground, yet three men died. Shortly after takeoff, *Challenger* and all seven members of the crew were destroyed. Most recently, just minutes from returning home safely to the cheers and waiting arms of loving families, *Columbia* and all seven crew members were lost. Interestingly, from what is normally thought of as the birth of space travel—the launching of *Sputnik 1* on October 5, 1957—to the tragedy of the *Columbia* on February 1, 2003, it is believed that only twenty-two people have died in space-related accidents (seventeen Americans and five Russians).

## An Embedded Problem

Over a year after the *Columbia* tragedy, Washington released other news concerning the space program. Apparently, many spacecraft within the fleet may have flown for more than twenty-five years with some of the gears in the two-part tail rudder installed backward. Not only that, some spare parts were also found to have the gears reversed. The consequences for this oversight could have been deadly.

Within hours of the loss of the *Columbia*, NASA formed the *Columbia* Accident Investigation Board (CAIB). Headed by Retired Navy Admiral Harold Gehman, Jr., the CAIB spent nearly seven months reviewing evidence, talking to engineers, conducting experiments, and trying to re-create the incident in simulated and controlled situations. When the board's report was released in August 2003, it concluded that the culture that had developed over several years at NASA was primarily to blame for the loss of the *Columbia*.

Many of the indicators of that culture could also be traced back to the *Challenger* incident some seventeen years earlier. As Paul Recer of the Associated Press reported, "These repeating patterns mean that flawed practices embedded in NASA's organizational system continued for 20 years and made substantial contributions to both accidents."[1]

In summarizing the CAIB report, Recer wrote, "NASA mission managers fell into the habit of accepting as normal some flaws in the shuttle system and tended to ignore or not recognize that these problems could foreshadow catastrophe."[2] Recer went on to note that the report stated that the biggest issue was "ineffective leadership" that "failed to fulfill the implicit contract to do whatever is possible to ensure the safety of the crew."[3]

## An Obvious Problem

The 1995 movie *Apollo 13*, starring Tom Hanks, Kevin Bacon, and Bill Paxton, made famous another true space story. The mission went well during the six-day flight from April 11 to April 17, 1970, until the vastly understated message came over the radio, "Okay, Houston, we have a problem here."

We would later learn an oxygen tank had exploded, severely damaging the service module and actually leaving the command module without power or air. A great scene in the movie takes place shortly thereafter when the flight director at mission control announces, "I want everybody to alert your support teams. Wake up anybody you need. Get them in here.... Let's work the problem, people. Let's not make things worse by guessing."[4] He would go on to say, "Gentlemen, I want you all to forget the flight plan. From this moment on, we are improvising a new mission."[5]

"I WANT EVERYBODY TO ALERT YOUR SUPPORT TEAMS. WAKE UP ANYBODY YOU NEED. GET THEM IN HERE.... LET'S WORK THE PROBLEM, PEOPLE. LET'S NOT MAKE THINGS WORSE BY GUESSING."

In the next few hours and days, some pretty remarkable things took place. The result was the safe return of three astronauts: James A. Lovell, Jr., Fred W. Haise, Jr., and John L. Swigert, Jr.

I find it interesting that the three tragedies that took place in NASA's manned flights were the result of relatively minor problems compared to what was experienced by *Apollo 13*. Yet in those three tragedies, a total of seventeen lives were lost. In the case of *Apollo 13*, three astronauts were safely returned to their families, and all three men continued to be a part of the program they dearly loved and for which they had risked their lives.

My observations are in no way intended to minimize the tragedies of *Apollo 1, Challenger*, or *Columbia*. But I think it is relevant to understand that in such a valuable and complicated program, loss of life can occur at any stage—whether on the launchpad, during liftoff, or within minutes of an anticipated successful landing. Likewise, opportunities exist at all stages to acknowledge a problem and take corrective, lifesaving action.

## Three Periods of Disaster

Unlike the space program, some things in life are not rocket science. Over the years, as I have looked at the need for rites of passage into adulthood within the church family, I couldn't help but picture all our sons and daughters. What we are facing in our families and churches is very similar to the history of our nation's space program. When I began to understand the statistics pertaining to the loss of our young men and women from the church, it became quite apparent that many are lost during the prelaunch phase prior even to getting to the launchpad for adulthood. Second, we lose many right after launching them into adulthood—as we fall prey to wishful thinking about their preparation and readiness. And last, many who were in the church through high school and as they headed off to college or the workplace are lost just moments before landing safely in the body of believers.

Yet it was also interesting to note that in more than forty years of space travel on the part of the United States, only three incidents have taken the lives of American astronauts. All three occurred at different flight stages—one at prelaunch, one immediately after launch, and one at reentry. Note that no astronauts have ever been lost during the main segment of the mission in space.

## Ask the Hard Questions

If we were to reevaluate the space program and assume for a moment that we had lost 30–40 percent of our astronauts at the prelaunch state, 50–70 percent of those remaining immediately after launching, and that upon reentry—thinking everything was safe—we were likely to lose nearly 90 percent of our remaining astronauts, I wonder if we would deem that program to be successful. How long would it be allowed to exist with that much loss of life?

Within the youth programs in our churches across the United States, however, we find those types of statistics. No one seems to question the facts, yet there does not appear to be an outcry from the church across America, and most parents admit they just don't know what to do at this point.

Week after week I speak with parents and youth workers. In nearly every case, I am told the same thing: Youth programs are working; our youth are getting stronger by the day. Yet the reality is that parents and youth workers readily admit that by the time their kids reach age thirteen or fourteen, a battle has already begun. Many parents openly admit it is all they can do to keep their kids in church each week. One district youth director told me his churches don't even target teens after their sophomore year in high school. The effort required doesn't equal the payoff, so they focus on kids in junior high and the first two years of high school.

> ONE DISTRICT YOUTH DIRECTOR TOLD ME HIS CHURCHES DON'T EVEN TARGET TEENS AFTER THEIR SOPHOMORE YEAR IN HIGH SCHOOL.

## Don't Accept the Abnormal

As a dad who—by my own admission—has been less than perfect, I have often felt I was in a battle to pass on my faith to my children and see them live their lives with similar values. I see similarities between the assessment NASA received and the condition of Christian families and churches today. Over the years we have accepted things as normal that are not normal. We have allowed repeated bad habits to imbed themselves in our families and churches. This truth is not new; it has simply been clouded over by changes in our culture.

Unlike the approach taken by the flight director of *Apollo 13* when he stated they were to forget the flight plan and instead improvise a new mission, we still have the same mission for our children that God gave us from the beginning. Now is the time for parents to quit improvising and get back to the original flight plan—God's.

Help started for *Apollo 13* when the crew said, "Okay, Houston, we have a problem here." Today we might begin by simply stating, *"Okay, God, we have a problem here."*

## FOR PERSONAL REFLECTION OR GROUP DISCUSSION

1. What space-program disaster stands out the most in your memory, and why?

2. What phase of life would you consider your children to be in: the prelaunch phase to adulthood, on the launchpad to adulthood, or in the postlaunch phase of early adulthood?

3. Which of these phases is more worrisome to you as you think about helping your children successfully reach adulthood and keep their own faith? Why?

4. Do you recall you and your friends struggling to stay in church? If so, which phase did you find most difficult: the prelaunch, launch, or postlaunch phase?

5. Why should we be saying/praying, "God, we have a problem here"?

## CHAPTER 3

# Two Down and One to Go!

The thought of losing another generation from the church doesn't even register with most Christians in America. We are essentially unaware that we have lost or are in the process of losing not just the two prior generations, but also the current generation of teens. Most of us are so wrapped up in our daily lives that we are oblivious to the changes that have occurred from our parents and grandparents to the current generation of young people.

We have a tendency to be taken in by the media sensationalism of our culture, while we miss the everyday happenings that are far more damaging and threatening to the church and to our families. This can best be seen by yet another tragedy—one of a totally different nature from the space shuttle tragedies referred to in chapter 2.

## A Terrible Tragedy

On April 20, 1999, two young men walked into Columbine High School in Littleton, Colorado, less than two miles from my home. Within a relatively short time, the casualties included twelve students and a teacher, Dave Sanders. We often forget that the real loss of life on that day was *fourteen* students and a teacher—because the parents of Eric Harris and Dylan Klebold also conducted funerals and buried sons. I'm not sure we will ever be able to measure the total number of casualties from the Columbine tragedy. In the months and years following the incident, there have been other deaths directly or indirectly attributable to Columbine, as well as several "copycat" incidents that have taken place. Countless lives have been forever changed.

My family and I were at the graduation ceremony for the Columbine High School class of 2002—significant in that this was the last class made up of students who attended Columbine at the time of the shootings. The principal, as well as many of the teachers, had made a decision to stay with this class and see them through until their graduation. Many teachers who had planned to retire earlier decided after the tragedy to remain until the final class graduated. That really speaks volumes about the teachers and staff at Columbine.

Many times in the days and weeks following the shootings, my family and I would walk through Clement Park and the parking lot adjacent to Columbine High School. It was there that the news reporters set up camp. I remember counting as many as fifteen different RVs that had been converted into news platforms for news agencies within the United States and from around the world. People across America would see the news being broadcast from makeshift studios established in that parking lot. Memorials spontaneously appeared in the park for each one of the fallen students and for Dave Sanders, their teacher.

The Columbine tragedy wasn't the first incident at a school involving students shooting and killing their classmates, nor would it be the last. Every now and then we hear about such plots being uncovered, fortunately, prior to any action being taken. It's difficult to imagine anything worse than students killing students and the loss of life at such a young age.

But there is, I think, a far greater tragedy taking place across our nation, though it lacks sensationalism and national news coverage. It also lacks, in many cases, the attention of those who could make the most difference or have the greatest impact for change. This tragedy is the loss of our young men and women from our church families. Day by day and hour by hour, it appears that our sons and daughters are making deliberate decisions to abandon the faith of their parents, their families, and the structure of the church as we know it.

## We're Losing Generations

Thom Rainer, in his book The Bridger Generation, did us a great service by analyzing the four most recent (at the time of his research) "generations." For statistical analysis, he referred to the Builders, those born before 1945; the Baby Boomers, those born from 1946 to 1964; the Baby Busters, born between 1965 and 1976; and the Bridgers, born between 1977 and 1994. After researching hundreds of churches, Rainer stated, "At presentrends, we will reach only 4 percent of the Bridgers for Christ."[1] His conclusion is that we are losing an entire generation. The following percentages demonstrate the decreasing portion of each of these four generations being reached for Christ.[2]

| ESTIMATED PROPORTION OF EACH GENERATION REACHED FOR CHRIST | |
|---|---|
| Generation | Percentage Reached for Christ |
| Builders | 65% |
| Boomers | 35% |
| Busters | 15% |
| Bridgers | 4%* |
| * Based on present trends among older Bridgers | |

While I agree with Dr. Rainer's assessment that we are losing an entire generation, when I look at the statistics he presents, I am compelled to suggest that we have already lost *two* generations and are in the process of losing a third. Although I admit I haven't been trained in statistical analysis, it seems to me that when more of a generation is against us than for us, we have, in fact, lost that generation.

It isn't difficult to apply this logic to the information presented by Dr. Rainer. The strength of our nation in the Builders generation can be seen in that nearly two-thirds of that generation were reached for Christ. Unfortunately, however, the numbers dwindle from there. Without trying to sound too alarming, when those numbers are extrapolated to the next generation, whom can we expect to reach in the generation following the Bridgers?!

The current generation of young people has taken many names, depending on whom you ask. Josh McDowell refers to this generation as the "Disconnected" generation; Dawson McAllister refers to it as the "Millennial" generation; George Barna refers to it as the "Mosaic" generation. Regardless of the name attached to this group of young people, the results of recent studies are the same. We have nearly lost this generation, and this appears in actuality to be the continuation of the loss of the two preceding generations—all with very little notice and fanfare. Referring to the Bridger generation, Rainer wrote,

> WE HAVE NEARLY LOST THIS GENERATION, AND THIS APPEARS TO BE THE CONTINUATION OF THE LOSS OF THE TWO PRECEDING GENERATIONS— ALL WITH VERY LITTLE NOTICE AND FANFARE.

> By far the simplest explanation for the churches that have not reached the Bridgers is ignorance, or lack of awareness. Many church leaders simply do not realize that they are losing a generation. A number of them have youth ministers and active youth and children's programs. But the activities and programs often disguise the churches' failures to reach the Bridgers.[3]

Josh McDowell began an urgent message in his newsletter with two quotes. The first was from Dr. Howard G. Hendricks, chairman of the Center for Christian Leadership: "If we don't act soon, we may lose a whole generation."[4] The second quote was from Ron Luce, president of Teen Mania Ministries: "We need nothing short of a spiritual revolution to see a generation become passionate followers of Christ."[5]

McDowell himself then stated,

> In all my forty years of ministry, I've never known an issue more dominant than what is presently on the hearts and minds of today's youth leaders and parents.
>
> I continue to hear one dominating and reoccurring theme. It is what the vast majority of youth leaders and parents now identify as their number one priority.

In fact, it is as if every youth leader in the country woke up this morning and said the same thing: "I fear that my kids will spend their childhood and teenage years in the church and walk away unchanged."[6]

In *The Battle for a Generation*, Ron Hutchcraft wrote,

Even secular researchers realize the critical situation our kids are in. Several years ago, some major research was done on American teenagers. The researchers were so alarmed by their findings that they titled their report "Code Blue." When my wife was in the hospital for surgery recently, the button next to her bed had those two words over it. In a medical environment, a "Code Blue" is a summons to all personnel that this is a life-or-death emergency—one for which everyone drops what he or she is doing to respond. That is how the researchers described the desperation of American teenagers. Drop everything … respond quickly … this is life-or-death.[7]

## Decision Time

Frankly, I believe the church has two choices. We can continue doing business as usual, and the numbers will speak for themselves. Or we can say, "Okay, God, we have a problem," and acknowledge that to get home safely we're going to need some help. I believe this second response reflects the heart cry of parents across our nation. In many ways we have just tried to continue doing the same things better, hoping the problem would go away. Yet, as we can see by the numbers, the problem hasn't gone away; and many families feel they have lost their sons and daughters from the church and from the faith they hold so dear.

In my thinking, parents need two questions answered. First, how did we get where we are today? (We're looking at this question in the first part of this book.) And, second, do we really know where we want to go? (That's the question we'll take up later in this book.)

## Where Are We?

Over the course of serving twenty-three years in the United States Army, I was never lost; but I certainly was disoriented at times and not absolutely sure of my actual location. This was important because in all those cases I was headed to a specific destination. In fact, others were depending on my being at a precise location. Taking it a step further, as an officer, others were depending on me to get them to the right place at the right time. On any occasion in which I became disoriented, two questions arose: "Exactly where am I?" and "Where do I need to go?"

To determine my precise location, it helped to replay how I had arrived there. I never had a GPS (Global Positioning System) to tell me exactly where, within a few feet, I was located. Rather, I was limited to a map, a compass, and visual efforts to identify the terrain features or environment in which I found myself.

It might be helpful for leaders and parents in the church to do the same thing. First, we need to ask, "Where are we? How did we get to this point in our churches and our families?"

I realize we can use statistics to try to prove or disprove just about anything. I'm sure many of us have listened in sheer amazement during political campaigns when both sides used the same statistic to try to make their point. In short, statistics are just that—statistics. It's the analysis and application of those statistics that make them important for us. And when statistics come from many different sources and studies and draw the same conclusions, it would be prudent for us to give them some serious consideration.

In studying various reports from many sources, including Robert Simonds (Citizens for Excellence in Education), Josh McDowell (Josh McDowell Ministry), George Barna (Barna Research Group), and Focus on the Family, we find a consistency in the information and a continuity in the conclusions being drawn. From all of these sources—along with my own personal interviews with youth pastors and parents across the nation—I have concluded several things:

- ⦿ Of the children born after 1985 who were in the church at the time of starting kindergarten, the church will lose 70–80 percent of them by high school graduation.

- The greatest loss will occur beginning at the ages of thirteen and fourteen, and will reach a disastrous peak during the ages of fifteen and sixteen.

- Of the young men and women who are in the church at the time of their graduation from high school, we will lose more than 90 percent of them within five years, with the greatest loss coming within the first two years after graduation.

Some may feel that the numbers simply reflect the fact that many of our kids head to college and are not in church during that period. Unfortunately, current trends indicate that once our kids go off to college, they aren't coming back to church—except to visit their parents.

Something else really strikes me as significant. So many of us parents drifted away from the church in our teen and post-teen years and then came back to the church later. Typically we came back after having our own kids. Though we think that's normal, in truth there's nothing normal about drifting away from the church.

**THERE IS NOTHING NORMAL ABOUT LEAVING THE CHURCH TO FIND YOUR ADULTHOOD.**

I believe the problem is that very few of us, if any, were launched into adulthood by our church or family before leaving the church as youth and deciding to come back as adults. Frankly, most Christian parents know there's a problem but just can't zero in on it. So, until we can figure it out or hear the truth, we allow ourselves to feel like it must be normal. But there is nothing normal about leaving the church to find your adulthood. It wasn't right for us when we were young, and neither should it be viewed as acceptable for our kids.

## The Bottom Line

So what do these conclusions really mean to us as parents? The reality is that if you look back at one hundred children in the church beginning kindergarten together, by the time they graduate from high school, we will have lost seventy to eighty of them—leaving us with just twenty to thirty of the original hundred. Then in the next five years, and particularly within the next two years, we will lose

90 percent of those remaining young adults. We are retaining only about 3–4 percent of what God entrusted to us as families. If your family is in that category—with all your kids still in church and walking in their faith—you may find it difficult to accept these statistics.

"YOU KNOW, I THINK I'M THE ONLY ONE FROM MY YOUTH GROUP WHO IS STILL IN CHURCH."

However, most parents I talk to readily identify with the numbers, regardless of whether their kids are in church, because they realize they are in a battle and they need help.

It is also important to understand that what I'm talking about is not evangelism but stewardship of a generation. If we as the church can't get it right with our own sons and daughters, how can we expect to reach the sons and daughters of those who have never even been presented with a credible offer of the gospel? Putting it another way, why would God trust us with the lives of others when we have failed so dramatically to be good stewards of what he has already given us?

Again, I realize statistics can be used and abused. Yet in nearly every venue in which I have spoken during the last six years (which includes more than twenty different denominations or church fellowships in more than forty states and several foreign countries), pastors, youth pastors, and parents have told me the numbers hold true in their church.

Let me give you one example. Last year, in a small town in North Carolina, I was introduced to the young, married daughter of a local pastor. After she asked me about my ministry and I shared with her these kinds of statistics and conclusions, she thought for a moment and then said, "You know, I think I'm the only one from my youth group who is still in church."

It really doesn't matter what the statistics are. We just need to ask some hard questions: As churches and families, how are our kids doing? Are they still in church because they want to be—with their own vibrant faith? Or are they merely attending "Mom and Dad's church" and listening to "Mom and Dad's pastor"? In reality, are they only two weeks away from leaving the church?

# FOR PERSONAL REFLECTION OR GROUP DISCUSSION

1. In what way did the Columbine tragedy affect your family?

2. To what extent do you identify with Josh McDowell's characterization of the concerns of the American church's youth leaders and parents: "I fear that my kids will spend their childhood and teenage years in the church and walk away unchanged"?

3. How do you feel about the sobering scenarios presented in this chapter about the loss of youth from the church?

4. How effective is your church in keeping its young people?

5. Did you drift away from the church in your teen and post-teen years and then come back to the church later? What are the risks associated with this pattern?

6. Do you think your children feel they are merely attending "Mom and Dad's church" and listening to "Mom and Dad's pastor"? If so, what would it take for your kids to feel that your church is also their church?

# IF YOU THINK *YOU'RE* CONFUSED

The concept of adulthood isn't confusing at all—that is, unless you take time to think about the indicators throughout our society as to what constitutes an adult in any arena!

## Signs of Confusion

I had an interesting conversation several years ago while staying in a motel in Louisiana. Before leaving to minister on a Sunday morning, I walked past the outdoor swimming pool. It was January and the pool was closed, but the sign was still very prevalent. Rule Number 4 indicated that "all children must be accompanied by an adult" to swim in the pool.

Upon entering the lobby, I asked the desk clerk at what age a young person would be "adult enough" to swim in the pool without a parent's supervision. She gazed at me with a strange look—after all, it was a cold day in January, the pool was closed, and my family wasn't with me—and then asked why I wanted that information. I responded that it might actually be something I would want to preach about.

The desk clerk laughed. After pausing for a moment, she said, "Well, it's not written down anyplace." I suggested, then, that they were probably just covering themselves in the event of a lawsuit, which she agreed was the case. So I asked, "At what age do *you* think a young person becomes adult enough to swim alone?" She replied that, in her opinion, a young person would be an adult for the sake of swimming in the pool at age thirteen. Then, without taking a breath, she went on to add, "But I wouldn't consider them adults for anything else."

I had a second question. I had noticed a cigarette machine in the lobby. A sign was posted on it that said, "All minors are forbidden to purchase cigarettes." As I pointed toward the cigarette machine, the desk clerk responded—before I could finish my question—"Age eighteen." I replied, "I imagine that's written down." She smiled and said, "Yes, that's the law."

Looking to the other side of the lobby, I saw a set of large wooden doors that opened into a lounge/bar area. A sign posted above those doors said, "Minors are forbidden to enter due to gaming devices inside." Again, this presented an interesting question for me, so I asked what that sign meant. She said, "Well, actually, our sign is wrong because we don't have any gaming devices inside."

"If the sign *was* right, what would it mean?"

The clerk very carefully laid out the legal implications of that sign for adulthood. She began by stating that since they don't have gaming devices there any longer, a young person could go inside at the age of eighteen and play pool, but he or she had to be twenty-one to buy alcohol. But if they decided to put gaming devices back in (which they were licensed to do), then a young person would have to be twenty-one to get a drink *or* to play pool.

I looked at her and said, "Let me see if I have this right. At this motel in Louisiana, young people are adult enough to drown themselves in the pool at age thirteen. But if they want to kill themselves with cigarettes, they have to be eighteen to be adult enough for that. And if they want to beat somebody with a pool cue as an adult, they can do that at eighteen—provided there are no gaming devices in the room; otherwise, they must wait until they're twenty-one. And in any event, they can be an adult for a drink at twenty-one, whether there is a gaming device in the room or not."

The woman looked at me with a smile and said, "You've got it. Who says men don't listen?!"

## State-Sanctioned Confusion

It seems to me that it would be only mildly confusing if all states adhered to the same laws or guidelines when it came to the issue of adulthood.

One time I was speaking in Idaho but staying in a hotel across the state line in Oregon. The laws in the two states concerning adulthood were actually different for just such things as the use of pools and hot tubs. In one state you were considered adult enough to be in the hot tub by yourself at age thirteen; but if you crossed the state line, you had to be fifteen to be adult enough to use the hot tub. Think about this for a moment: You could actually step across the state line and lose your adulthood for two more years. Easy come, easy go.

Everywhere around us, we have indications of the age adulthood begins—most of which are contradictory and confusing. These are designed primarily with one purpose in mind: to protect the institution that places the sign. In the United States, the confusing issues of adulthood and the age for attaining adulthood can be divided into three general categories of restrictions or stipulations: in the use of facilities and similar privileges, in the food and entertainment industry, and in the legal arena. Let's look at the lack of clarity and consistency in these three areas of our society.

> YOU COULD ACTUALLY STEP ACROSS THE STATE LINE AND LOSE YOUR ADULTHOOD FOR TWO MORE YEARS.

I've already mentioned examples of limiting young people's use of facilities (e.g., swimming pools, hot tubs, fitness centers). We also see licensing restrictions for hunting, fishing, and driving a car or motorcycle. We can begin to understand how easy it is for young men and women to perceive that adulthood is like a carrot on a stick. Society will extend it to them when it is to society's advantage and will withdraw it from them when there is no perceivable gain on behalf of society.

## Kids and Restaurants

Concerning the food and entertainment industry, there appears to be one overriding goal: Consider young people adults as early as possible so you can charge them adult prices! Most restaurants allow children under the age of ten or twelve to order from a children's menu. Above that age, a young person is declared to be an adult and ineligible for the children's menu. My point is not to debate the validity of being able to order from a children's menu, but to highlight the arbitrary factors used to determine at what age a person becomes an adult.

On a somewhat humorous note, there may be inconsistencies even within the same establishment. I went to a buffet with a pastor and his family after services one Sunday. The sign stated that ten-year-olds and under would pay the children's rate. So the pastor had to pay the full adult fare for his eleven-year-old son. At the dessert bar there was another sign that spoke to the issue of adulthood. It pronounced, "All children under the age of twelve are required to be accompanied by an adult to get dessert." While this might seem confusing for most, the message I heard was that we must monitor our children's choices. They are adult enough at the age of ten or eleven to serve themselves green beans, carrots, chicken, and roast beef; but when it comes to things like carrot cake, lemon meringue pie, and chocolate chip cookies, they need supervision! Since I had just given a message at the pastor's church about the confusion we have in the United States regarding the issues of adulthood, his facial expression said it all!

## Kids and Media

The movie-rating system, which many people believe to be mandatory and legally binding to the theaters, is actually a voluntary system designed to assist parents. In truth, theaters are under no obligation whatsoever to enforce the rating system.[1]

Let's look at what the rating system really means and the implications for the concept of adulthood. The basic ratings today are G (general audiences—all ages admitted), PG (parental guidance suggested—some material may not be suitable for children), PG-13 (parents strongly cautioned—some material may be inappropriate for children under thirteen), R (restricted—under seventeen requires accompanying parent or adult guardian), and NC-17 (no one under seventeen admitted).

Movie ratings, which first began in 1968, were originally comprised of G (general audiences—for all ages), M (mature audiences—parental guidance suggested), R (restricted audiences—under eighteen must be accompanied by an adult), and X (no one under seventeen admitted). Revisions made in 1984 separated the PG rating into the two categories of PG and PG-13. Finally, in 1990, two more revisions were made. The movie industry began to give a brief explanation of why a film received an R rating, since, in the opinion of the ratings board, R-rated films contained "adult material." The motion picture industry felt that such explanations would help parents determine whether a film was appropriate for their children. It was also at this time that the X-rated category, which "appeared to have taken on a surly meaning in the minds of many people," was changed to NC-17.[2] Any movies now rated NC-17 would have been rated X under the old system.

One may wonder what all of this has to do with the issue of adulthood in general, and for defining adulthood as it pertains to rites of passage in particular. The fact is that as the movie industry rates films from PG to PG-13 to R to NC-17, it has stated that adulthood begins at age seventeen or eighteen. At eighteen a person is allowed, by his or her own choice (and the movie theater's voluntary submission to the rating system), to watch a film that previously would have been rated X for explicit sexual content. When a movie is rated R for sexual or violent content, the explanation will often state that the film contains "adult situations" or "adult themes." Doesn't this communicate that the vocabulary of adults will normally include vulgarities or cursing and that the lifestyle of the typical adult is pornographic and violent?!

If you really want to be confused as a parent, combine the movie-rating system with the television-rating system. The TV system doesn't start with a simple G rating, but has three ratings before we even get to a G. The first rating is Y, given to a program that is "designed to be appropriate for all children." This is followed by Y7 for "children age seven and above." Then we get to Y7FV, which denotes

IF YOU REALLY WANT TO BE CONFUSED AS A PARENT, COMBINE THE MOVIE-RATING SYSTEM WITH THE TELEVISION-RATING SYSTEM.

ograms where fantasy and violence may be more intense or more combative."[3]

Further adding to the confusion, the TV networks don't use the PG-13 rating. Instead, they have chosen TV14 to identify programs that contain one or more of the following: intense violence (V), intense sexual situations (S), strong coarse language (L), or intensely suggestive dialogue (D).

Finally, instead of R and NC-17, the television industry lumps everything above TV14 into TVMA. This category is for a "Mature Audience Only." The description states that a TVMA program is "specifically designed to be viewed by adults and therefore may be unsuitable for children under 17." Such programs contain one or more of the following: graphic violence (V), explicit sexual activity (S), or crude indecent language (L).[4]

A movie could be rated R or NC-17, but on TV it would carry that rating and TVMA. A PG-13 movie could be shown on TV as TV14. The movie and TV industries have supposedly put ratings on movies and shows to help us parents. Do you feel "helped"? I often tell parents that we are being ambushed by the film and television industries. But the industry will vehemently deny any confusion in the ratings and go back to the fact that they state their ratings are just *guides* for parents.

In 2004 researchers reported, "Children who watched a lot of TV with sexual content were about twice as likely to start having intercourse during the subsequent year as those who had little exposure to televised sex."[5]

Parents need to understand that our own children want good and workable definitions for "adulthood" and related issues of life. When we can't or won't supply them, our kids turn to the sources that completely saturate their lives—movies and television. Do we really want the media defining adulthood for our children?

## Kids and Courts

When it comes to establishing a legal definition of adulthood, the sword doesn't swing both ways. If a young person—by behavior, discipline, and responsibility—functions at a level commensurate with what is perceived as necessary to be an adult, he or she is still legally regarded as a child until age eighteen. But if a young person violates the law or commits a crime, in the majority (85 percent) of states in our country, legislatures and prosecutors determine at what age that individual is tried as an adult rather than as a juvenile.[6] Sadly enough, the decision in most cases is based on the severity of the crime and, I believe, whether or not the prosecutor believes he or she can win a conviction.

In the case of severe crimes, we typically see young people being tried as adults; and year by year we see an ever-increasing number of juveniles being tried as adults. The U.S. Department of Justice reported in 1997, "An analysis of the NCSL (National Conference of State Legislatures) results makes clear that the States are continuing to move quickly to expand adult court jurisdiction over juvenile offenders."[7]

When comparing various states and their handling of youth and adults, the judicial system is inconsistent and confusing. In some states, like New York, "16- and 17-year-olds are automatically processed as an adult regardless of the crime, because the juvenile court's jurisdiction ends at 15."[8]

As one article stated the situation, "In most legal definitions, a child becomes an adult at age 18. But the age at which a child becomes an adult in court can vary."[9] Lionel Tate was convicted of first-degree murder at the age of fourteen and sentenced to life in prison for a crime he committed at age twelve. Had Lionel Tate been a terrific student and all-around great kid, he would have had to wait until he turned eighteen to be an adult.

> IN SOME STATES, LIKE NEW YORK, "16- AND 17-YEAR-OLDS ARE AUTOMATICALLY PROCESSED AS AN ADULT REGARDLESS OF THE CRIME, BECAUSE THE JUVENILE COURT'S JURISDICTION ENDS AT 15."

## Who Determines the Definitions?

It is clear that in a wide range of circumstances, the term *adult* is used throughout society in differing ways. Whether in a restaurant, at a theater box office, or in a courtroom, there is absolutely nothing consistent—either in form or function—concerning the use of the word *adult* as the defining characteristic. There does not appear to be within our societal structure one place with an understanding of adulthood that can serve as an anchor point for parents and their children.

The issue is not about launching into a debate regarding the age-appropriateness of movies or at what age a person should be legally charged as an adult. The real issue for parents is simple: Who do we want to define adulthood for our children? Did God just leave this one up to us, or does he have answers on this subject?

## FOR PERSONAL REFLECTION OR GROUP DISCUSSION

1. This chapter recounts numerous confusing, and sometimes amusing, examples of the various ages when young people are considered adults. What other examples have you seen?


2. How have you used the movie and TV rating systems in your family? How helpful have you found them to be?


3. In what way, in your opinion, has the film industry been able to "change the conscience of our nation"? How true is this for the Christian community?


4. What influence has the entertainment media (movies, TV, music) had on the values and behavior of your kids?


5. Do you know at what age, in your state, a young person can legally be charged as an adult for a crime?


6. From this chapter, what's the most important point to share with your children?

## CHAPTER 5

# THE (MUCH) LONG(ER) ROAD TO ADULTHOOD

If we are unsure whether the mixed messages about adulthood throughout our society are confusing, we need only to pick up a local newspaper. In May 2003, the University of Chicago announced the results of its study on American perceptions of adulthood.[1] Referring to this study, headlines in newspapers throughout our country said things like "Adulthood Comes Later These Days,"[2] and "Becoming a Grown-up."[3]

Martha Irvine of the Associated Press began by saying, "The law may imply that you are a grown-up when you are old enough to vote, serve in the military, or legally drink alcohol; but most Americans really think adulthood begins at age 26...."[4]

Columnist Tom Perry of the *Green Bay Press Gazette* reflected on the study: "More than most other Western nations, we're all over the map with our definitions of adulthood.... At 18 a person can vote, enter into legal contracts and serve in the military. Of course, a person can't legally drink until he or she is 21, even if he or she is deemed old enough to fight for our country in Iraq."[5]

Perry went on to point out the dichotomous nature of our laws and definitions when he wrote, "At the same time, if a 15- or 16-year-old commits a murder, he or she most likely will be tried as an adult."[6]

How is it that in America—perceived by many to be the most advanced nation in the world—we can be so confused on the issue of adulthood? The answer to that question can perhaps best be seen in examining the concept of adolescence. It is this period that Marilyn Gardner referred to in her article titled "The Longer Road to Adulthood." From a societal standpoint, she stated that "adolescence is a period of no-longer and not-yet—a time of being no longer a child but not yet an adult."[7]

## The Invention of "Adolescence"

The concept of adolescence, as it is used today, is relatively new. Let's look at the invention (and I really do mean the *invention*) of adolescence. The father of adolescence is widely accepted to be psychologist G. Stanley Hall of Worcester, Massachusetts. In his foundational piece, *Adolescence*, written in 1904, Professor Hall invented the current-day understanding of adolescence. As Laurence Steinberg, professor of psychology at Temple University and author of a leading college textbook on adolescent development, observed,

> For Hall, the development of the individual through these stages is determined primarily by instinct—by biological and genetic forces within the person—and hardly influenced by the environment.
>
> The most important legacy of Hall's view of adolescence is the notion that adolescence is inevitably a period of storm and stress.... Because this turbulence is biologically determined, it is unavoidable.[8]

It was this acceptance of G. Stanley Hall's work that led to the widely accepted belief that our children must go through a period of rebellion and crises before entering the adult world. Based on what many believed to be foundational truths arrived at by careful research, it became widely accepted that the turbulence of adolescence was inevitable.

Dr. Hall's studies and opinions were embraced initially by the educational community, which transmitted them into American families, and from there to our churches—a perfect example of allowing the culture into the church instead of taking the church into the culture. A close study of the educational systems within our churches (Sunday school, adult education, and so forth) gives us an understanding that those programs are modeled after the educational processes and structures utilized in our public education system.

G. Stanley Hall suggested that adolescence is a period of time commencing with the onset of puberty until adulthood and is "suggestive of some ancient period of storm and stress."[9] Hall's alleged findings can be summarized as follows: (1) Adolescence is a crisis time in the life of all children that they have no choice but to go through, due to hormonal and other changes in their bodies; (2) more than just anticipating these types of changes and this period of rebellion and confusion, parents should expect and even condone and work with this adolescent period because it is normal and natural; and (3) environmental conditions cannot alter the inevitable storm.

Many people before and after Hall have tried to convince the world that their findings are scientific and accurate. Many have accepted the writings of Hall and others, such as French philosopher Jean-Jacques Rousseau, as factual. This has resulted in a situation along the lines of a remake of an old movie where everyone was convinced the world was flat.

The truth is starting to resurface, and as parents, we should be relieved. The battle lines are being drawn by the fact, as Steinberg points out, that "although neither Hall nor Rousseau had any scientific evidence that adolescence is any more stormy than childhood or adulthood, their portrayal of teenagers as passionate, fickle, and unpredictable persists today."[10]

## The Church's Endorsement of "Adolescence"

Even today, if parents claim their teenager is not having problems, not struggling, not going through an identity crisis, or not being in rebellion, most other parents look at them as if they are naïve and don't truly understand what is going on. In 1984, Youth for Christ published a significant book that became a manual for parents and teenagers: *Parents and Teenagers: A Guide to Solving Problems and Building Relationships*. The book was a compilation of articles by more than seventy-five noted contributors, such as Bill Bright, Tony Campolo, Evelyn Christenson, James Dobson, Leighton Ford, Richard C. Halverson, Howard Hendricks, Jay Kesler, Grace Ketterman, Gordon

MacDonald, Josh McDowell, Adrian Rogers, Marshall Shelley, and Chuck Swindoll. Billy Graham wrote the foreword.

The introduction included a section written by Ray and Anne Ortlund titled "Meeting the Challenges of Adolescence." The Ortlunds began by saying, "We parents go along for years in a comfortable parent-child relationship, the one we've always known, and then suddenly—when the kid is about twelve, about to enter junior high—everything changes. It's a crisis point, the beginning of the move into adulthood. It's a challenge we've never had before, so we ourselves have to behave differently as well as relate differently to our child."[11]

PICK ANY BOOK WRITTEN ABOUT THE TEEN YEARS, WHETHER WRITTEN BY A CHRISTIAN OR NON-CHRISTIAN, AND THOSE YEARS WILL BE DESCRIBED AS TIMES OF CRISIS, TURMOIL, AND REBELLION.

Pick any book written about the teen years, whether written by a Christian or non-Christian, and those years will be described as times of crisis, turmoil, and rebellion.

It is important to see the progression or the change that has taken place over the years. G. Stanley Hall identified the adolescent period as being between thirteen and eighteen. We can conclude that the lengthened road to adulthood has not been because of a longer period of childhood. In fact it is just the opposite. Studies indicate that kids are maturing much younger. They are being marketed to at a much younger age. Credit card offers are being mailed to teens, and parents are actually getting those credit cards for their children. Many of the indicators of adulthood are being allowed or forced on our children at a much younger age, apparently to the satisfaction of unwitting parents and ministry leaders.

## The Effects of "Adolescence"

Because of the ever-widening abyss called adolescence, childhood is being shortened and the road to adulthood lengthened.

Dr. Donald Joy described adolescence as it is understood today: "Remember that adolescence refers to the time gap between sexually ripening (average age of twelve for girls and thirteen for boys) and the privileges of adult work and marriage (average age of twenty-five for males' first marriage today)."[12] Dr. Joy contended, "We invented adolescence. We decided that kids were a liability, that they were a luxury."[13] Concerning the impact of this within the church, Joy asserted that "the invention of adolescence in our culture is crippling most of our young before they embrace the third decade of life."[14]

Already we can observe the conflict within the Christian community concerning this issue of adolescence. In one camp we see an ever-growing number of individuals who view the concept of adolescence as a human-invented curse placed on our children with the expectation of rebellion, confusion, and loss of identity. These folks refuse to accept the ill-founded notions that storm and stress are biologically natural and that environment is not a factor in a young person's development. On the other side of the battlefield, many Christian leaders and educators view a stormy adolescence as a normal process and cycle within the life of every young person.

> "THE INVENTION OF ADOLESCENCE IN OUR CULTURE IS CRIPPLING MOST OF OUR YOUNG BEFORE THEY EMBRACE THE THIRD DECADE OF LIFE."

As a parent you have a choice to make. You must decide if God desires you to be a parent during these years, or to give up, give in, and let the world raise your kids.

I realize that anyone venturing to speak out about the wrongful existence of adolescence runs the risk of appearing to be speaking against some of the greatest Christian "giants" of our day. Dr. James Dobson of Focus on the Family published a book in 1978 titled *Preparing for Adolescence: How to Survive the Coming Years of Change*. This book was a careful study of the concept of adolescence and what it brings to society as well as to the church. Dr. Dobson's message was essentially this: Adulthood contains inherent privileges and responsibilities; adolescence is a period of time in which the responsibilities of adulthood are placed on those who are no longer perceived to be children, but who are not yet accepted as adults with the rights that go with those responsibilities.

I contend that privileges and responsibilities go hand-in-hand. When the responsibility comes without the rights, we can certainly expect rebellion, confusion, and a time of crisis.

Many educators and parents have confused the human-bestowed privileges of adulthood with the God-bestowed state of adulthood. At some point both boys and girls are going to become adults, whether or not they act like adults according to our standards.

## Lessons from History

We can examine the history of adolescence to see what it has actually done to society, primarily in the United States, and as a result, to the church in the United States.

Adolescence was once thought to start around age thirteen, which was also the initiation of puberty, and continue to about age eighteen. Eighteen was determined to be the age at which young people would leave state-required schooling and choose a vocation. For some that meant heading off to college; for others it meant entering a trade, and for many young women it meant embracing the roles of wife and mother.

**MANY EDUCATORS AND PARENTS HAVE CONFUSED THE HUMAN-BESTOWED PRIVILEGES OF ADULTHOOD WITH THE GOD-BESTOWED STATE OF ADULTHOOD.**

We have watched as the time period of adolescence has been pushed out to approximately twenty-three years of age, which is about the time young adults finish college and go into full-time employment. As indicated in the study done by the University of Chicago in 2003, people now perceive that adulthood begins around the age of twenty-six. And Donald Joy pointed out that he has watched many young people maintain the adolescent mentality until almost their thirtieth year.

Even as the end of adolescence is pushed further out, the onset occurs at a much younger age. Part of the blame for this shift lies with parents who want their children to grow up faster, as demonstrated by the adult behaviors some permit or even encourage in their children. An example of this is the sophisticated way some girls are allowed to dress.

Historically, the concept of adolescence didn't really catch on until the 1950s. In that period after World War II and the Korean Conflict, our nation experienced economic expansion and growth with an increased emphasis on education and educators. It was during this time that the concepts of adolescent mentality and behavior became widely accepted in the culture and, as a result, in the church. We also saw during the 1950s the growth of youth ministry—initially incorporated by volunteers—starting at the high school level and then moving down to the junior high level.

Without a biblical basis, how could a concept like adolescence become widely accepted within the church? Part of the blame lies within our education system. There is often little difference between the curriculum used to train Christian psychologists and that which instructs secular psychologists.

The best example of this was brought to my attention a few years ago when my son took a required course on human growth and development at the Christian college he attended. At the same time, my other son's girlfriend took a similar course at a state university. In my thinking, a course at a Christian college should be different from a course at a secular university. The tragic truth is that they both used the same textbook—and the same lesson plans, training materials, and tests provided by the publisher. There was no difference between how the Christian college and the state college taught this course on human development. The same was true for the course on adolescent development, which is required at both colleges for a degree in psychology or counseling.

Some may say this is making a mountain out of a molehill, and that these are merely observations from one of those overzealous, fanatical Christians who seek to isolate themselves from all those who don't believe as they do. But take a look at the introduction to the McGraw-Hill textbook on adolescence:

> The most important biosocial theorist was G. Stanley Hall (1904), considered the "father" of the scientific study of adolescence. Hall,

WITHOUT A BIBLICAL BASIS, HOW COULD A CONCEPT LIKE ADOLESCENCE BECOME WIDELY ACCEPTED WITHIN THE CHURCH?

who was very much influenced by the work of Charles Darwin, the author of the theory of evolution, believed that the development of the individual parallels the development of the human species, a notion referred to as his theory of recapitulation.[15]

## Fostering Parental Fear

The image conveyed by Christian psychologists and psychiatrists who talk to us about preparing for adolescence is one of preparing for a tropical storm. Most books on adolescence warn us to approach it as if we were storm chasers: We need to understand why it takes place and what atmospheric conditions create it, but we must also realize there is not one single thing we can do about it except prepare for it when we see it on the radar screen. In effect they're telling parents, "Batten down the hatches, board up the doors and the windows, stock up on food and water, and get the generator ready—because this is going to be a time in which there is no control, and the only thing you can do is ride it out."

In my research on the subject of rites of passage, the greatest gain has been an understanding of the impact this issue of adolescence has had on society. This chapter on adolescence really only scratches the surface. More study is needed in order to understand the source, definition, and implication of adolescence on the Christian community, and on future generations if this is not changed.

The dangers of the concept of adolescence were perhaps best summed up by Lance Morrow in a *Time* essay following the massacre at Columbine High School:

Humans ... have turned the long stretch from puberty to autonomy into a suspended state of simultaneous overindulgence and neglect. American adolescence tends to be disconnected from the adult world and from the functioning expectation (the hope, the obligation) of entering that world and assuming a responsible place there. The word *adolescence* means, literally, growing up.... Without adult connection, adolescence becomes a never land, a Mall of Lost Children.[16]

The training most Christian adults have received leads them to regard adolescence as a stage they'd rather not go through. They'd rather have Peter Pan and Tinker Bell take their children away to Neverland and bring them back when they are self-sufficient, independent adults.

## FOR PERSONAL REFLECTION OR GROUP DISCUSSION

1. How does our popular culture define adulthood?

2. In two or three sentences, give your definition of adulthood and at what age it naturally begins. How do you communicate your definition to your children?

3. Do you agree with the author's assessment of the "invention of adolescence"? Why or why not?

4. If adolescence has no biblical foundation, how has the concept distorted and negatively affected true adulthood?

5. What have the church and Christian leaders communicated about adolescence? Has this primarily fostered feelings of fear or encouragement?

## CHAPTER 6

# WE WILL JUST HAVE TO DO IT FOR OURSELVES

Without a specific destination or clearly defined route to that destination, travelers have a dilemma. They have to decide for themselves where they're going and how they're going to get there. The loss of adult connection within our churches and society has resulted in just that situation for this generation of young people.

The lack of adult connection has left our own sons and daughters without a road map to adulthood.

### Filling the Void

I vividly remember visiting the headquarters of a ministry that had its genesis in the Columbine shootings—a group of young men and women who travel around the country speaking to young people. (There is no one over the age of twenty-one involved in the ministry.) As I stood in the hallway, I noticed on the wall a photograph of what appeared to be several hundred young men and women being prayed for by others in the group. I asked the person I was with what the photograph represented. Without hesitation he replied, "We are simply praying our fathers' blessing."

I pondered that for a moment and looked again at the young people in the photo. I couldn't see anyone who appeared to be over twenty-one, so I asked, "Who were the fathers there that prayed that blessing?" He smiled and said, "There were none. We just realized the hole in our hearts and the need we had to be blessed by our fathers. And without them there, we just did it for ourselves."

They understood the blessing and the empowering they needed from their fathers; so in the absence of those fathers, they set their own rules and simply prayed for one another.

Not long after that, I was riding in the car with my sons and one of their friends. The Christian high school they attended didn't have dances like the public schools, but the school did have a fall and spring formal affair, which prompted the dating or pairing up of couples. I had determined some years earlier that, before the date, I would have the privilege, honor, and responsibility of interviewing any young women whom my sons would go out with on an occasion of this nature. I had done this the two previous years, but for the event that had just taken place I had been convinced by both my sons that the girls they were going with were just friends and that they had paired up just to have dates for the function. Without realizing the implications, I had acquiesced to not interviewing the girls.

As we drove along, my sons told me that both the girls felt slighted because they had known of and anticipated the interview process. They felt I didn't think enough of them to take the time to interview them. I realized then that I needed to talk to both young women to try to correct their perceptions, and I needed to acknowledge that I had made a mistake and apologize for it.

> "THERE WERE NONE. WE JUST REALIZED THE HOLE IN OUR HEARTS AND THE NEED WE HAD TO BE BLESSED BY OUR FATHERS. AND WITHOUT THEM THERE, WE JUST DID IT FOR OURSELVES."

That wasn't the most significant part of the conversation, however. My sons' friend who had listened to all of this finally made the comment, "Well, no one cares about who I go out with. But I like that interviewing idea; I guess I'll just have to start doing that myself!"

We laughed, and I told him I would be happy to interview any girl he wanted to go out with. What he was really saying was that he didn't feel anyone of the older generation cared enough about him to take the time to help shape and give guidance to what was happening in his life. I will also say that I know the young man's dad, and he worked hard at being a good dad. He just didn't know his son's need in this case.

## "Extreme" Initiations

Donald Joy told the story of a phone call he received on an Easter morning a few years ago from a woman who had been notified at 4:30 a.m. that her son and his friend were in the emergency room at Baylor Hospital. While her son had significant injuries and was initially categorized as being in "serious" condition, he would walk out of the hospital less than a week later under his own power. His buddy just had a few abrasions, but his neck was broken and his spinal cord seriously damaged—he would never walk again.

The two young men had been involved in a deadly game known as "chicken" or "showdown" at two in the morning on a back road. After consuming alcohol, the drivers and their buddies in two cars—with headlights off—would approach each other from opposite directions. The rules were simple: The first to turn away would render the other one the victor. It seems that at the last moment, the woman's son, instead of hitting the other car head on, had turned away and struck a tree.

Dr. Joy concluded, "It was a ritual of risk and potential mixing of blood and steel, connecting testosterone to yearning for dominance, for passing the test of initiation. 'Becoming a man' required some suitably challenging ceremony. His buddies defined the rules of the game."[1]

What's happening across the nation appears to be simple in its basic nature. The lack of an adult connection—that is, men and women of the older generation helping to define the rules and bring value to their lives—has caused our sons and daughters to make the rules up as they go. The most tragic situation occurs when, desiring acceptance, they allow others to define the rules for them.

This "extreme generation" is a generation in search of meaning and significance for their lives. They are trying to figure out what is "enough" personal value, self-worth, or significance. In their search for value, young people have become "extreme" by trying to push their lives to the limit. The problem is, accomplishments don't last, and soon the young person has to push harder against new limits to feel valuable.

If we don't give our young people rites of passage that convey their value, they'll create their own rites of passage—or others will do so for them.

In many ways, this reality has been around for a long time. Jeff Brodsky wrote this:

> During my research I was shocked that the only people not doing anything in this area were modern Christians! We do nothing to help our boys understand the responsibilities and joys of passing on to manhood. And we fail to celebrate the passing on to womanhood for our girls. There's no rite, no celebration, no ceremony—nothing![2]

IF WE DON'T GIVE OUR YOUNG PEOPLE RITES OF PASSAGE THAT CONVEY THEIR VALUE, THEY'LL CREATE THEIR OWN RITES OF PASSAGE—OR OTHERS WILL DO SO FOR THEM.

It may seem logical to research the various rites of passage into adulthood taking place around the world and try to transfer those in some meaningful way into our churches or our culture. While it would be interesting and certainly enlightening to study the ceremonial processes that were developed, for instance, in Africa, the Far East, or Australia, I don't think we can expect such rites to have optimal significance in the lives of our children. This certainly isn't meant to discount or discredit the value of those ceremonies and the importance of those traditions within those cultures, but merely to transplant those ceremonies and traditions into churches across the United States would have less value for our culture.

## Gang Initiations

It is important to understand the types of rites of passage that already exist in our culture and are being used to try to fill the vacuum in the lives of our youth. One such initiation occurs within gangs across our nation.

Several years ago, the National Counseling Resource Center in Rochester, Minnesota, published a handbook for clergy, youth workers, and parents titled *A Handbook on Youth Violence and Gangs*. What it revealed about the initiation rights for gangs confirmed what I had been told by gang members. The primary initiation right is called the "beating in" or the "beating down." The gang members form either a circle or two lines (much like a gauntlet), and the new "wannabes" either enter into the center of the circle or walk between the two lines. In either case, the current gang members mercilessly beat the initiates to the ground. If a female is joining the gang, the initiation will most likely involve her having sex with members of the gang in the middle of the circle or as she passes between the two lines.[3]

> "IF WE COULD GET THROUGH THIS, WE WOULD FINALLY BE ACCEPTED FOR WHO WE ARE."

A good friend called to tell me he realized what I had been saying about gangs was true. He lives in an upper middle-class neighborhood and personally has very little to do with gangs in his area. But he supports a ministry in an urban environment that attempts to help youth leave their gangs. My friend listened as a staff member spoke to a young gang member about the practice of beating in. He asked why he would allow that to be done to him. The young man stated that he knew it would be very hard, but he and his fellow initiates also knew that "if we could get through this, we would finally be accepted for who we are."

Hearing this brought tears to my eyes because it again made me realize that what the church was neglecting to do—receive young men and women with love—their own peers were doing with violence. And it didn't matter that it was extremely painful; their need for acceptance at any cost led them to submit to this type of initiation.

## Athletic Initiations

It doesn't take extensive research and surveys to identify rites of passage already incorporated into our everyday lives. One needs only to look at sports teams at all levels—whether that be junior high, high school, college, and even professional—to see that there is normally some sort of an initiation rite associated with them. Those initiation rites can go from the very sacred to the very brutal, often resembling gang-type initiations.

In 1998, the news media reported what it called an "inner-city gang-like" initiation that took place during the training camp of the New Orleans Saints football team. In the hotel where the players were staying, the veterans lined up along a hallway, and the rookies were required to "run the gauntlet." When the story first broke, some made it seem to be a racially motivated incident, since the players who received the most injuries were white. Further investigation revealed that the incident had nothing to do with skin color. It was simply an initiation required of all rookies. The tragedy of this story was that one of the promising linemen suffered a detached retina, and another player required stitches as a result of apparently being thrown through a glass window.[4]

We've all heard similar stories. Research indicates that initiation rites in organized sports at every level are far more the norm than the exception. Many school clubs and almost all fraternities and sororities have some type of entrance initiation to try to add value to being a part of their organizations. An ESPN story published in 2002 stated,

> Considering that an Alfred University survey found that 80 percent of college athletes had been hazed, the vast majority of hazing incidents—on the high school, college and pro levels—go unreported. Nonetheless, incidents that eventually gain the attention of the news media have increased steadily since 1980, when the abuse of athletes by athletes first began to receive public attention.[5]

## Student Initiations

Unfortunately, the most dangerous initiations are not those that are organized or structured. The tremendous death toll over the years from college students' drinking has gone largely ignored. In October 2004, *USA Today* reported that "binge drinking" had recently taken the lives of five students, and that was "just the tip of the iceberg." The article cited Henry Wechsler, a Harvard researcher who suggested that the actual toll was approximately fourteen hundred student deaths per year when you factor in alcohol-related deaths due to falls and automobile accidents.[6]

As I taught a seminar at a military base on the issues of adulthood, and specifically manhood, I watched one of the base commanders seem to ponder and process these types of initiations. At the conclusion of the seminar, he stated that he now understood what had taken place at the beginning of the school year. It was reported to him that on the first day of classes at the middle school, which consisted of fifth and sixth graders, the new sixth-grade guys formed two lines, and the new fifth-grade guys were required to run through the lines while being struck as they tried to get from one end to the other. Any boys who refused to go through the line were chased down and beaten.

## Positive Examples

Mature adult leadership sets an entirely different tone in initiations or rites of passage. While many examples exist, I think a couple of the brightest are the Boy Scouts and Girl Scouts. Several differences stand out in the way these men and women guide the youth through the stages and seasons of their lives.

The first is that the rules are clearly established. The requirements for every rank and achievement are published, and there is honor associated with each one as well. One of the most striking characteristics of that system is the very open and public desire of the leaders to see each scout reach the highest level possible. The young men and women are not really competing with one another, as there are no limits or quotas on the rank. In actuality, they compete with themselves to be the best they can be. I'm convinced the adult connection is what makes the difference.

My son experienced two different initiation rites—one that had an adult connection and one that did not. When Chad made the varsity soccer team in his freshman year at a small Christian high school, he was required by the other players to go through an initiation of sorts. It consisted of spraying shaving cream all over my son's head and shaving him! The reality of the situation was that, while Chad's ego was bruised a little, he was not physically harmed in any way; and at the conclusion of the ordeal he felt he had passed the test and now was a part of the varsity team.

The contrast to that came when Chad played college soccer. In his sophomore year the coaching staff instituted an initiation rite for the new players who had been selected for the varsity team. Though this initiation involved the players, it was led and guided by Christian men—and not just any men, but the coach and the assistant coach, who used the opportunity to instill honor and manhood in both current and new players.

The initiation began with the current varsity players going into the rooms of the newly selected players at approximately midnight and blindfolding them—but at the same time assuring them that they weren't going to be harmed and encouraging them to trust their "kidnappers." They were then led to the soccer field, and the jerseys they would wear as varsity players were placed on the grass in front of them. When their blindfolds were taken off, the new varsity players found themselves standing behind their new jerseys. Then the coaching staff and the current players spoke to each guy about the privilege, honor, and responsibility of playing on the varsity team of that college. They spoke blessing and empowerment and honor into their lives, and then one by one prayed for them and presented their jerseys to them.

I'm sure the majority of the varsity players who participated in that initiation rite had only known previously of rituals involving shaving cream and shaving heads. It wasn't until mature adult men connected with them that they were able to understand the importance and experience the power of a proper rite of passage.

## Learning from Elephants

Several stories have been reported about a program in the Pilanesberg National Park in northwestern South Africa. It seems that all the older male elephants had been killed off, and the younger male elephants, left to themselves, had formed into nothing short of roving gangs that would indiscriminately kill other animals they came in contact with. The game wardens in the area were unsure of what to do. Someone suggested they bring in older elephants from another area, which they did.

The results were amazing. In a very short period of time, the older male elephants took charge of their younger counterparts and actually trained them as to how a male elephant should act. The gangs of young elephants were immediately broken up, because it was far more important to the younger elephants to be accepted by the older elephants than it was to be accepted by their peers and to allow their peers to define the rules for them.[7]

> THE ABSENCE OF RITES OF PASSAGE LEADS TO A SERIOUS BREAKDOWN IN THE PROCESS OF MATURING AS A PERSON.

The absence of rites of passage is not limited to Christian families and churches. As we struggle with the issues of how best to launch our children into productive adult lives, we find that the concept of rites of passage and the need to recognize significant times in the lives of our children is universal in nature and transcends cultures and geopolitical boundaries. The *Encyclopedia of World Problems and Human Potential* declares that the current lack of rites of passage is an urgent global problem:

> The absence of rites of passage leads to a serious breakdown in the process of maturing as a person. Young people are unable to participate in society in a creative manner because societal structures no longer consider it their responsibility to intentionally establish the necessary marks of passing from one age-related social role to another, such as: child to youth, youth to adult, adult to elder. The result is that society has no clear expectation of how people should participate in these roles and therefore individuals do not know what is required by society.[8]

The conclusion to be drawn from this is fairly simple. In the absence of an adult connection that could have established the guidelines and requirements for conduct and acceptance into society, the young people of this generation have been forced to establish their own rules, determine what is right for themselves, and establish their own initiation rites. This is not only true in society as a whole but in the church as well.

# FOR PERSONAL REFLECTION OR GROUP DISCUSSION

1. What formal or informal initiations have you experienced in your lifetime? Do you recall each initiation as being uplifting or somewhat degrading?


2. What formal or informal initiations have your children already experienced? How would you describe them?


3. Why do you feel young people today go to extreme, even brutal, measures in some of their initiations?


4. Chuck shares a couple of positive examples of initiations (other than in the church). Can you think of others?


5. Why do you suppose churches in America, with rare exception, don't engage in rites of passage for their youth?

## CHAPTER 7

# "A Great Place to Raise Kids, but a Terrible Place to Raise Adults"

Several years ago I visited a good friend who had just spent some time in the small town where he had grown up. He told me about an incident that happened while he watched a youth soccer game with old friends. As he looked around at the beautiful, plush soccer field and the nearby school and houses, he made the comment, "I had forgotten what a great place this is to raise kids." Without a moment's hesitation, his lifelong friend—who still lived in that town—replied, "Yes, but it's a terrible place to raise adults."

The moment I heard that statement, I couldn't help but apply it to the church today. Though the church is a great place to raise kids, it has, in fact, become a terrible place to raise adults. I know we don't want to believe that. We would prefer to look idealistically and optimistically at the church, which we affectionately call our "family."

The fact of the matter is that a closer look at the church reveals indications of how we got to this position and why the church is struggling. It's been reported that more than 85 percent of Protestant churches in America have reached a plateau or are in decline at this time. As stated in chapter 2, we will lose approximately 70–80 percent of our young people who were in the church when they started kindergarten by the time they get to high school graduation. In addition, we will lose in excess of 90 percent of churchgoing high school graduates within five years of their graduation. To reiterate: It appears that we are only reaching and keeping approximately 3–4 percent of this generation, as compared to 65 percent of the Builder generation.

Several factors must be considered.

## Separation of the Ages

The first issue is that of stratification. While we call the church a family, in reality our ministries are stratified by age groups or special needs. And the special needs often relate to a portion of an age group—for example, special needs within the sector of the seniors, Baby Boomers, or Baby Busters. Typically all the generations of the church are brought together for one worship service throughout the week, and even on that occasion, in many churches the children are removed for a separate worship service away from their parents.

Mark DeVries, associate pastor for youth and families at First Presbyterian Church in Nashville, Tennessee, identifies the problem well. Several years ago I had the opportunity to visit with Mark, and he gave me a copy of a book he wrote in 1994. In the first chapter he stated, "What I am calling 'traditional youth ministry' has little to do with style or programming or personality. It has to do with the place of teenagers in the community of faith. Over the last century, churches and para-church youth ministries alike have increasingly (and often unwittingly) held to a single strategy that has become the most common characteristic of this model: the isolation of teenagers from the adult world and particularly from their own parents."[1]

When it's announced that the church family is going to watch a movie, it normally means that those identified as adults are going to watch a movie in the sanctuary; the youth will watch that movie or a different one in their facility, and the children will watch a children's movie in their part of the building.

Often we think that because we're heading to the same place together, we're really involved in each other's lives. Most church functions would resemble a reunion rather than a true family gathering. Larry Kreider, founder of Dove Christian Fellowship International, stated it this way:

There is a huge difference between vibrant family life and an extended family getting together for a reunion. When family comes together for a *reunion*, they present their best side to the larger family.... Real family knows the struggles because they are there day after day.... Real family knows each other inside out. They see the good, the bad, and the ugly, and they still love each other and work as a unit to encourage each member. We can be ourselves in a family. There is no test to pass; we are included simply because we are *family*.[2]

## The Reality: A Church Within the Church

We have lost the adult connection our young men and women need to transition smoothly into adulthood. This would further explain why the time period of adolescence is being extended. In a growing number of churches, the youth program is virtually the only ministry that is not just allowed but encouraged to become its own church. My observations are based on interviews and contact with several hundred churches of various denominations across the nation.

Many youth pastors are being directed not even to call their ministry a youth ministry, but to call themselves by a separate name as a youth church. One youth pastor approached me before I spoke and asked me not to use the title "youth ministries," because they had worked for more than two years to take that term out of their vocabulary. They were in the process of helping the larger church understand that they, in fact, were a separate church and that this was the healthiest thing for the youth. The church was in the process of constructing and staffing a separate building—all the time wondering why the young men and women weren't transitioning with clarity into adulthood and moving into the other ministries of the church.

Many church leaders have been convinced that to have a viable, thriving youth ministry, the youth must have a separate facility—either

IN A GROWING NUMBER OF CHURCHES, THE YOUTH PROGRAM IS VIRTUALLY THE ONLY MINISTRY THAT IS NOT JUST ALLOWED BUT ENCOURAGED TO BECOME ITS OWN CHURCH.

within the church building or, in many cases, completely separate from that structure.

## The Result: Christians Without a Church

The youth church is no longer a ministry within the church but functions in the capacity of a separate church for everything except finances, for which it is still tied to and supported by the home church—with no adult connection except for a few leaders. As the young men and women graduate from the youth church, there is absolutely no place for them to go. In churches across America, because we have allowed our youth groups to become churches, when young people graduate from high school, they also graduate from their parents' church. That accounts, to a great extent, for the huge reduction in attendance for that age group during the next five years of their lives. And since they have not been accepted as adults in the body of believers, most young people will use the expression "Now that I'm on my own" when they are living away from home—even though their mother and father may be paying for the tuition, room and board, and so forth.

WHEN YOUNG PEOPLE GRADUATE FROM HIGH SCHOOL, THEY ALSO GRADUATE FROM THEIR PARENTS' CHURCH.

Tragically, in many cases we are seeing youth ministries and campus ministries inadvertently discipling young men and women right out of the local church. If young people finally see themselves as adults, they will associate their current faith experience with adulthood and their earlier experience with childhood. Therefore they don't see a need for a local church in their lives.

And the majority of young men and women in our high school and junior high youth groups don't perceive themselves as going to their family's church, except in the context of youth group. They see the "big church" as Mom and Dad's church, where they go to listen to Mom and Dad's pastor. *Their* pastor is the youth pastor, and *their* church is their youth group or Sunday school class, at best. So once again we see the scenario that when they graduate from high school—if they are still even in the church at that point—they will often graduate from church with no place to go. In talking with youth leaders across the country, I find that the few young folks who remain in the church normally do so because they have been called to be interns or placed in leadership positions.

## And the Beat Goes On

Many churches have established viable college and singles ministries. But the problem still persists that there is no connection with the adult world as we know it. As I talked about this at a church on the East Coast, several of the staff and one of the associate pastors smiled, and this pastor told me I wouldn't believe what had just taken place in their church: the dynamic of stratifying the church and establishing a church within the church for each of those age groups.

Some time earlier they had established a college-age ministry, primarily because parents demanded something be done to keep their kids in church. They hired a pastor for the college-age group, up through about age twenty-six or twenty-seven. They found, then, that at that age most of the young people were out of college and in their first jobs, but they still weren't connected with the congregation and the church was still losing them. They either wanted to stay in that group or they wouldn't come to church at all. The church made a decision to have the associate pastor for the college-age group create a new church that would go from about age twenty-eight to thirty-five. Then they hired another pastor for the college age.

A fellowship that has the size and the resources to hire pastors for all the different age groups may appear to be a growing church, but typically there is a lack of spiritual continuity that allows a believer to flow smoothly through the seasons of life and truly identify with the church as a whole as opposed to just one ministry of the church.

Furthermore, we see a hands-off approach to youth ministry as youth departments are allowed or encouraged to develop their own budgets, their own missions programs, their own praise and worship teams, their own small groups, their own discipleship programs, their own mentoring programs, and so forth. In fact, peer mentoring is a rapidly growing concept in youth ministry. While clearly there is a place for peer mentoring or peer counseling—where young people who are going through a crisis or specific situation can get help from peers who have had a similar experience—it seems to me that the majority of mentoring should be done by experienced mentors who are more spiritually mature and chronologically older than the young person being mentored.

## What Are We Preparing Our Kids For?

The military system repeatedly emphasizes in its promotion ceremonies that a promotion doesn't occur just because of good performance in the current grade, but is primarily based on the potential for performance at the level of promotion. Therefore it is incumbent upon commanders and supervisors to train and equip their people for that next level of service if they expect them to be successful.

IN MOST CHURCHES THE PRIMARY FOCUS IS ON HELPING CHILDREN TO BE GOOD CHRISTIAN CHILDREN, AND TEENAGERS TO BE GOOD CHRISTIAN TEENAGERS— WITH NO CONNECTION TO SET THEM ON A PATHWAY TO BECOMING SUCCESSFUL, SOLID, CHRISTIAN ADULTS.

We don't necessarily find this happening in the local church. In fact, it appears to be just the opposite. In most churches, the primary focus is on helping children to be good Christian children, and teenagers to be good Christian teenagers—with no connection to set them on a pathway to becoming successful, solid, Christian adults.

Mark DeVries shared the story of a young woman who had been a vibrant part of the youth ministry at his church when he left for seminary, but who was inactive by the time he returned. Mark stated, "Apparently after leaving our active youth ministry, she had not been impressed with any of the churches in her new city and chose not to get involved in any of them. She has graduated from college and, after living with her boyfriend for awhile, is now on the fast track toward success in her career. Although she looks back on her youth experience nostalgically, she has little interest in pursuing her faith as an adult."[3]

Mark went on to capture in one sentence the relevance of this example: "The important aspect of Jenny's story is that our program *succeeded* in leading her to become a mature Christian *teenager*, but somehow failed to place her on the track toward mature Christian *adulthood*."[4] Frankly I believe we have misidentified the real crisis. The crisis is not simply that our own kids are leaving the church. That is only a symptom of the crisis. I would echo Mark DeVries's assertion that the real crisis facing our churches and families is that we are not leading our own children to mature Christian adulthood.

Young men and women who have been exposed to the gospel believe they are Christians and have faith—they just don't feel the need for the church as an active force in their lives. Specifically, my personal interviews with youth leaders and parents have led me to the conclusion that after young men and women get their driver's license, a significant percentage decides not to attend youth group.

In fact, I have come to believe that in many cases young people can be out of youth group for four to six weeks before their parents (especially Dad) will ever know. They leave the house at the same time with the same friends, so their parents assume they are going to youth group—not realizing they have decided to go someplace else. Eventually one of the parents will mention youth group, and the son or daughter's response will be, "I haven't been going to youth group for a long time." Although the parents are shocked, they often rationalize the situation and accept it as normal.

## So, What Is Normal?

Another problem is that parents, particularly those who are Baby Boomers, perceive it to be normal that during the period of so-called adolescence, people will drift away from the church, typically returning when they are married and have children. While that was the case for many current church attenders from the Baby Boomer generation, statistically that has not proven true for this current generation. In fact, just the opposite is true. They rarely come back to the church, because they have usually found "community" elsewhere. If and when they do come back, it is often only because they feel their children need the church for their moral development.

Again, we see that the church is a good place to raise kids but a terrible place to raise adults. Wayne Rice and David Veerman are two men with a great amount of experience working with teens and parents. They made the following observation:

> In today's world ... children don't become adults when they reach adolescence; they become teenagers. This poses a problem for both children and parents because no one really knows what a teenager is supposed to be. By default, teens themselves have created their own world apart from adults, and adults have chosen to just leave them alone. The long-term negative impact of the invention of adolescence has been the almost total isolation of adolescents from the people who can teach them the most—adults.[5]

It has been said by many that the biggest issue within the church today is that we fail to disciple our family members. While few might take exception to this statement and the importance of discipling within the body of believers, it also appears that the church is in decline because we, as a church family, are failing to provide spiritual continuity within the family of believers. There is no smooth transition from one season of life to the next. Instead of Christians and the church providing a model for the world, we have fit ourselves into the world's model, which says young people are in a season of fits and starts, not knowing where to go or what to do. "In time they will grow out of that and hopefully be productive members of society," we tell ourselves.

## The Growth of Youth Ministry ... and Stratification

Christ called us in Matthew 28:19 to "go and make disciples." Isn't it obvious from that statement that God is calling the church to help develop mature Christian believers, adult believers who are capable of reproducing? It appears the church has reversed the process to the detriment of the family members. The majority of the emphasis seems focused on making good Christian kids in children's ministry and youth ministry, but not transitioning them into adulthood.

This chapter is in no way meant to be a condemnation of youth pastors. My personal experience is that the heart and dedication of youth pastors and leaders is nothing short of phenomenal. With the odds stacked against them, and often with very little spiritual and emotional support from parents and churches, they go to war every day on behalf of our children.

The growth and change in youth ministry over the years gives us a stark picture of what has taken place. Many in the Builder and Baby Boomer generations remember the real beginnings of youth ministry. The surge in youth ministry, or youth groups, began in the 1950s—after World War II and the Korean War. We saw many dramatic changes at that time, both in our society and in our church culture.

THE REAL CRISIS FACING OUR CHURCHES AND FAMILIES IS THAT WE ARE NOT LEADING OUR OWN CHILDREN TO MATURE CHRISTIAN ADULTHOOD.

One of those changes was the new perception of the need for youth ministry within the traditional churches across our country. Originally most youth groups began as "senior high youth fellowships." Within a short period of time, churches recognized they were still losing their young people before they even got into senior high. Thus, youth ministry expanded to include junior high. In many smaller churches, the two were combined. Larger churches that could afford the staff or had sufficient volunteers did both.

Now we see churches specifically targeting students from junior high or middle school up through and including college-age young people. With each new ministry added, we lose more of the family concept of church and become more stratified. Day by day we see more individual congregations in the same church and less spiritual continuity for each believer. When it appears that we are losing an age group, we simply start a new program for them. But for Christian families to be successful, the church must be a great place to raise kids and a greater place to raise adults.

## FOR PERSONAL REFLECTION OR GROUP DISCUSSION

1. In what ways would you say your congregation is separated by age or need?

2. Would it be accurate to describe your youth or student ministry as "a church within the church"? If so, what downsides do you see in this type of program? If not, what is your youth ministry doing right?

3. As a parent, do you sometimes feel isolated from your children in your church? If so, what can you do to overcome the situation?

4. What effect on young people's involvement in church and youth group, if any, have you seen by their getting a driver's license?

5. When young people in your church graduate from high school, what percentage of them would you guess also "graduate" from the local church—and where do they go?

6. Does your church have a college-age or singles ministry? If so, would you describe those attending as separated from—or a viable part of—your congregation? What might be done to improve their sense of connection?

7. Do you agree that the focus of the church and Christian parents has become "helping children to be good Christian children, and teenagers to be good Christian teenagers—with no connection to set them on a pathway to becoming successful, solid, Christian adults"? If so, how can you change this focus?

# PART

## 2

# DON'T WE NEED TO KNOW WHERE WE'RE GOING?

# AND HOW WOULD YOU DESCRIBE IT?

During a ministry trip in the St. Louis area, I stayed with good friends Ray and Mary Morgan. One afternoon we went to a mall. Mary, who is an extraordinary shopper and can find bargains the normal eye cannot see, let me know which items were the best buys of the day.

One of those immediately caught my attention—bedspreads and comforters. My wife, Billie, had mentioned we needed some new bedding and if I saw a good deal to let her know. I grabbed my cell phone and called Billie back home in Denver to inform her of the awesome deals on three bedspreads I thought would be acceptable. Billie thought for a moment and then asked the killer question: "Can you describe them for me?"

That seemed like an easy question at first. I'm an educated, well-traveled man. Seriously, how hard can it be to describe three bed-spreads? So I began describing each of the bed sets with colors I was familiar with—red, green, blue. I could see a look of exasperation and frustration on Mary's face. Finally, after listening as long as she could to my ludicrous descriptions, she took the phone and began speaking to my wife in terms I had never heard before. It was as if they were speaking a foreign language!

When Mary and Billie finished talking, Mary handed my phone back and Billie said, "They all sound great. Mary will tell you which one we want."

Upon ending the conversation and putting the telephone in my pocket, I looked at Mary. She simply smiled, pointed to a set, and told me to tell the clerk that was the one we wanted. To this day if anyone asked me to describe our bedspread, I'd simply suggest they call my wife or Mary Morgan. I still don't speak that language, and I certainly can't describe it or define it for them. I like the bedspread, I just can't describe those types of items—not to a woman anyway!

## What Is "Adulthood"?

Now if you think that's funny, try asking five people in your church to define adulthood, and then ask five educators to describe adulthood, and then ask five young people what their perception of adulthood is and when they will get there. From those fifteen people you will probably get at least twenty different definitions, because after they hear the other responses, several of them will change their minds and their definitions.

> DO YOU THINK GOD IS WAITING TO DEFINE ADULTHOOD BASED ON WHAT PEOPLE SAY ON ANY GIVEN DAY AND HOW THINGS HAVE CHANGED OVER THE YEARS?

Much of the confusion about adulthood stems from the fact that over the years we have allowed the concept of adulthood to drift into some pretty murky waters. If you ask people what constitutes adulthood, you will get answers such as being self-sufficient, completing an education, getting married or starting a family, and moving out of the parents' home. You'll get all kinds of different factors, but none really define adulthood. In one of the primary textbooks on adolescence used at the university level, the author lists thirty-eight identifiers of adulthood. They range from financial independence to sexual issues.[1]

As I began studying adulthood, one thing became very clear to me. The church has lost the biblical pathway for defining adulthood. Perhaps that's why the *age* of adulthood can vary so much; it depends on how one chooses to define the *term* adulthood.

In many cases, a person being questioned about the definition of adulthood will ask, "In what context are you thinking?" I know this sounds awfully simple, but for a Christian, shouldn't there be a Christian answer to this question? Do you think God is waiting to define adulthood based on what people say on any given day and how things have changed over the years?

Think about the confusion that results when we use the characteristics of our society to determine adulthood. If getting married and starting a family is a mark of adulthood, does that mean the eighteen-year-old who is married and has a child and works full time to support his family is an adult—while the nineteen-year-old who is in college studying hard, making great grades, and volunteering at his church is still considered a child or an adolescent? Is the seventeen-year-old who commits a crime and is charged and tried as an adult to be considered an adult in our society—while the nineteen-year-old who doesn't commit a crime but works hard to be a productive member of society is still a child or an adolescent?

Do you see the traps we fall into when we allow the ever-changing winds of society to blow us to and fro on foundational spiritual issues?

> THERE DOES NOT APPEAR TO BE ANY PLACE IN THE BIBLE WHERE GOD INDICATES A PERIOD OF TIME WHEN A PERSON IS NO LONGER A CHILD BUT NOT QUITE AN ADULT.

## What Is God's Perspective?

In most churches where I speak, this is where the fun really begins. What seems to me to be the indisputable definition for adulthood from God's perspective cuts through the illogical, confusing, and circular thinking of the world. There does not appear to be any place in the Bible where God indicates a period of time when a person is no longer a child but not quite an adult. There is simply childhood and adulthood. In fact, the apostle Paul said in 1 Corinthians 13:11, "When I was a child, I talked like a child, I thought like a child, I reasoned like a child. When I became a man, I put childish ways behind me."

There is nothing in 1 Corinthians 13:11 that indicates there was a time period determined by society when Paul was no longer a child but not yet a man, nor when he was condemned by his Creator to a turbulent time of confusion and rebellion, seeking his identity, unsure of who he was and for what he was created. Quite the contrary is true: Once he was a child; then he became a man.

In the second chapter of Luke we see Jesus at age twelve, sitting in the temple courts among the teachers, listening and asking questions. At twelve, Jewish boys began to prepare to assume their place as members of the religious community at age thirteen. By the customs of the day, if Jesus had been three years old, he would not have been allowed to stay at the temple. If Jesus had been eight or nine years old, he would not have been allowed to stay in the temple. Yet, at twelve he was allowed to remain in the temple to listen to the teaching and ask questions.

How then do we find a biblical definition for adulthood? Let's try to see this issue through God's eyes. It seems that when God changes the body and makes it capable of reproducing life, God the Creator transforms the individual from a child to an adult. That is a tough pill to swallow for most of us because it opposes what we've been taught to believe within our society. Are you still having a tough time with this? Believe me, I understand, but I want to make sure you don't just blow past this without catching what I've said: Adulthood begins when God changes the body and makes it capable of reproducing life.

At this point I acknowledge that for some who may want to try to poke holes in the balloon before it lifts off, there are exceptions I cannot explain—and, frankly, can't wait to ask God about. Some young women begin their menstrual cycle very early, and some guys and girls never enter into typical puberty or adulthood. Perhaps a physically disabled person never develops the capacity to reproduce; that doesn't mean we don't consider him or her to be an adult. Do we as parents need to address such situations individually if they impact our children? Of course, but don't let the exceptions nullify the norm.

## A Personal Example

In 1971 I entered the United States Army at the lowest possible rank—a private. On that hot August day when I arrived at Ft. Leonard Wood, Missouri, I wore blue jeans, sandals, and a denim shirt. I didn't necessarily *look* like a soldier, but by law I *was* a soldier. I had raised my right hand, been sworn in, and accepted the responsibilities and privileges of serving in the United States Army.

Some would question whether I was an actual soldier at that point, but their questioning would be of a personal preference or biased nature. On the rolls of the United States Army, I was counted as a soldier. If you asked anyone who knew me what I was doing, his response would have been, "He's in the army; he's a soldier." Without a uniform, training, and formal testing, I was an unlikely candidate, but I was, in fact, a soldier at the very beginning stages.

> WITHOUT A UNIFORM, TRAINING, AND FORMAL TESTING, I WAS AN UNLIKELY CANDIDATE, BUT I WAS, IN FACT, A SOLDIER AT THE VERY BEGINNING STAGES.

After a few weeks of basic training, I graduated and was sent to advanced individual training. This was important because even though I had completed the basic training required for all soldiers, I still didn't have a military occupation specialty that would in turn give me a job and make me useful within the army. However, I was still a soldier. After completing advanced individual training and serving several months at Ft. Gordon, Georgia, I was given the opportunity to go to airborne training and then selected for Officer's Candidate School (OCS). Upon arriving at OCS at Ft. Benning, Georgia, I quickly realized that even though I had graduated from basic and advanced individual training and was a soldier with a military occupation specialty that could be utilized throughout the army, I still didn't measure up to their standard—because even with all the previous training, I had not graduated from airborne school, and therefore I was lovingly classified as a "leg."

In the months and years that followed, I would complete OCS, U.S. Army Ranger Training, and Army Special Forces Training, as well as other individualized schools such as scuba, jumpmaster, and Belgium Commando Training. In my twenty-three years of service in the United States Army, it became obvious to me that every day I served in the United States Army was a day that I should be growing and learning how to do my job better. Yet one thing was definite. From that hot day in August 1971 when I reported to Ft. Leonard Wood to my final day at Ft. Dix, New Jersey, when I retired twenty-three years later in 1994, there was not a day—regardless of the level of training I had received or where I was assigned to serve—that I was not considered a soldier.

## Don't Make It So Difficult

When we think about our young people, we realize some may still be in basic training, but shouldn't we still try to see them with God's eyes? Adulthood is not as complicated as we make it. In fact, from God's perspective, it appears to be quite simple. Again, when God the Creator changes the body and makes it capable of reproducing life, he transforms a person from a child into an adult. Interestingly enough, the more we study, the clearer the situation becomes. Whether you are studying human growth and development, adolescent behavior, psychology, sociology, or even biology, the changes that take place at what we call *puberty* mark the entry point into adulthood. In fact, the word *puberty* is derived from the Latin words *pubertas,* which means "the age or condition of physical maturity," and *pubes,* which means "a grown-up person, adult."[2]

WHY SHOULD OUR CHILDREN HAVE TO WONDER ABOUT SOMETHING THAT GOD HAS DECLARED TO BE SO?

I am reminded of a young man I met in Louisiana. At the conclusion of the rite of passage into adulthood, after he had received the blessing of his parents and the acceptance of his church as an adult, I asked him, "How are you doing?" With tears in his eyes, this young man of nearly eighteen said, "Incredible! Absolutely incredible! Since the day I turned sixteen, I have wondered when I could call myself a man and when anybody at my church would believe me."

As I held him in my arms and hugged him (yes, men hug too), I asked, "Are you still wondering?"

"No," he said. "Tonight, I know."

Why should our children have to wonder about something that God has declared to be so?

As a final thought—if you are still struggling with what I have been saying about adulthood—picture a father who is a terrific dad and Christian man. Imagine him and his thirteen-year-old daughter, who is definitely in the process of change. Visualize this father, his arm around his daughter, giving her a loving hug and telling her, "Honey, you know I love you and want the very best for you. These things that are happening to you and your b-b-body [such an easy word for a dad and a daughter at this age] are part of God's plan for you. It's like the caterpillar becoming the butterfly. But, honey, your father isn't quite ready for this, so I'm asking you to wait till you are eighteen to finish developing."

Of course, since she loves her father and wants to please him, she just decides to quit developing until she's eighteen so her dad can handle it. Oh yeah—that really works!

The fact is that no one but God is in control of this change. Not even the best of parents. As a result of not being able to control God's plan, we have changed the rules for adulthood by changing the definition to suit us. Helping our kids keep the faith as godly and responsible adults begins with returning to God's plan.

# FOR PERSONAL REFLECTION OR GROUP DISCUSSION

1. When you were a teenager, what were the markers for your having attained adulthood?

2. What are the characteristics and attributes our culture normally associates with adulthood today? In what ways have those affected your own thinking?

3. Read Luke 2:41–52. What do those verses communicate to you about the social status of Jesus at age twelve?

4. Do you agree that God's definition of adulthood is that time when he changes the body and makes it capable of reproducing life? Why or why not?

5. Do you struggle with your children, or any other children, being considered adults at age thirteen? If so, why?

## CHAPTER 9

# YOU HAVE GOT TO BE KIDDING ME!

Time and time again I have stood before congregations and asserted that adulthood is when God changes the body and makes it capable of reproducing life. Even after doing my best to present a logical, biblical case, I observe a look in their eyes that basically says, "You have got to be kidding me!" It's a look that says, "For some that may work at thirteen, but you don't know the kids I know. If you expect me to believe they're adults at age thirteen, you're going to have to work harder at convincing me."

At this point, I always ask the same question: "How many of you have a difficult time considering a thirteen-year-old to be an adult?" I ask for a show of hands. Invariably, 90 percent will raise their hands. Why is it that we can see from a biblical, biological, and psychological point of view that a person thirteen years old can actually be an adult, and yet have such a hard time believing and applying that reality?

## "Adulthood" vs. "Maturity"

The answer is simple: We impose something on the younger generation that we don't impose on our own generation or anyone older than ourselves. We require kids to be mature before they can be viewed as adults. This isn't a requirement for anyone our own age or older—just for the younger people.

When asked the meaning of maturity, people offer definitions that range from complicated to ludicrous. I recall sitting in a meeting with a group of parents who all agreed that our goal was to bring our children into spiritual maturity. I asked the group, "How would you define spiritual maturity?" To say there was a long pause is a gross understatement. Finally, one mother of two teenagers spoke up. "Actually, I don't think you achieve spiritual maturity in this lifetime. You are not really spiritually mature until God calls you home."

As her words hung in the room, the mother herself was one of the first to grasp the gravity of her statement. Placing her hands to her face, she exclaimed, "What have I been telling my kids?"

She got it! She realized in that moment that each time she had told her children they needed to be spiritually mature, she was simultaneously believing it was something they couldn't actually attain. Imagine the frustration of a young person who is constantly told he or she has to be mature by those who don't think the individual can make it.

Isn't spiritual maturity something that can be achieved in this lifetime? Isn't it something God points us to throughout the Scriptures?

I certainly don't want to make light of the importance of surrendering our lives to the Lord Jesus Christ. But if a person our age or older were to come into any of our churches having just destroyed his family, lost a business, and come out of a drug rehab program, and he were to fall facedown at the front of the sanctuary and ask Jesus Christ into his heart, we would all rejoice with him, and there would be no doubt this was an adult making an adult decision. At the same time, we would realize this same person has the spiritual maturity of an earthworm or less. While our own children, however, stand strong in their schools, go on mission trips, try to live good lives, and seek the Lord, we look at them and say they need to be more mature.

Why is it, then, that the man who fell facedown in the front of the church but is clueless when it comes to God's Word and applying God's principles to his life is accepted without question as an adult? If we were to question him in the presence of our own children, it would become obvious that he couldn't hold a candle to the maturity of our own kids; yet, we don't recognize it in them.

## Defining Maturity

If we are to separate maturity from adulthood, we must hold to God-given definitions of maturity and adulthood. Unlike the majority of people both inside and outside our churches who would base the definition of maturity on the actions of the individual, God's Word states that he looks at the heart.

Before defining spiritual maturity, let's go back and look at the message we convey to our children about maturity. I suggest that for the most part, spiritual maturity is defined by an older generation telling a younger generation to dress, act, and talk in a manner in which the older generation feels safe to be around. When we tell young people to grow up and act mature, aren't we really telling them we don't feel secure around them—that they scare us? We'd be quite comfortable if they would just speak, dress, and conduct themselves in a manner with which we feel comfortable. This understanding of spiritual maturity really asks our children to reproduce themselves in our image rather than in the image of Jesus Christ. Call it being hypocritical or pharisaical or phony—it doesn't matter which title we put on it, they all fit.

> I SUGGEST THAT FOR THE MOST PART, SPIRITUAL MATURITY IS DEFINED BY AN OLDER GENERATION TELLING A YOUNGER GENERATION TO DRESS, ACT, AND TALK IN A MANNER IN WHICH THE OLDER GENERATION FEELS SAFE TO BE AROUND.

## Looking to Jesus

So now, is there any scriptural support for separating maturity from adulthood? Let's go to the book of Hebrews and look at the life of Jesus Christ. We have already established that he was an adult when he sat among the teachers in the temple at age twelve. Yet he wasn't called into his ministry until he was about thirty. In speaking of Jesus, Hebrews 5:8–9 tells us, "Although he was a son, he learned obedience from what he suffered and, once made perfect, he became the source of eternal salvation for all who obey him."

Let's look at this passage closely and tie it to a following verse. This statement can really challenge our theology if we take it literally in its translated form, because what it seems to say is that after Jesus suffered through his obedience, he became perfect. Looking at that from the other side of the road would mean that prior to his suffering through obedience Christ was less than perfect. My personal theology—along with Christianity's theology for the last two thousand years—cannot buy into that reasoning.

Here is what we need to understand. First of all, Christ was in no way spiritually or morally imperfect. But it was his suffering that qualified him to be the perfect sacrifice on our behalf. Secondly, the Greek word that is translated in most of our Bibles as *perfect* is *teleios*, which means "mature," "complete," and "whole." God's Word tells us that although God's own Son was an adult, he still had room to be perfected as he lived his life and suffered here on earth.

I really like the way Eugene Peterson presented Hebrews 5:8–10 in *The Message*: "Though he was God's Son, he learned trusting-obedience by what he suffered, just as we do. Then, having arrived at the full stature of his maturity ... he became the source of eternal salvation to all who believingly obey him."

Throughout the Scriptures where the term *mature* is used, it is consistently identified as something that all believers can become. As we will see in a later chapter, maturity is a journey—not a destination.

## The Hebrews 5:14 Principle

How then do we define *maturity* so we can understand if we're on the right path? Later in the same chapter of Hebrews, the writer stated, "Anyone who lives on milk, being still an infant, is not acquainted with the teaching about righteousness. But solid food is for the mature, who by constant use have trained themselves to distinguish good from evil" (5:13–14).

The background of this passage is that God, through the writer of this letter, was warning the readers that they weren't growing in his Word and becoming mature. Verse 12 states that some of these believers ought to have been teachers by now but were not. In the early stages, a Christian needs milk—not solid food, not meat. But anyone who continues to live on milk, meaning the basic principles of the faith, remains an infant.

God tells us in verse 14 that solid food is for the mature. I love this device of Scripture where God then states "who by" and gives us a definition. He says, "But solid food is for the mature, who by constant use have trained themselves to distinguish good from evil." Some might believe that the distinguishing or discerning between good and evil is a spiritual gift that is given to some and not to others. God's Word says that for us to grow in the faith, we are to train ourselves to discern good from evil.

Let's wrap this up with a definition that we can apply to our lives today. For the purposes of our ministry and all teaching we do in any area, we define spiritual maturity, based on Hebrews 5:14, as follows: Spiritual maturity is reached when, through constant use of scriptural teaching and training and the power of the Holy Spirit, a person discerns good from evil and has the courage to act on the good and take responsibility for his or her decision.

## A Realistic Goal

I want you to think about that definition for a moment and then ask yourself, if this was the growth path my son or daughter was on, would I be satisfied? If you could look at your children, speak with them, and see that they were growing by being able to distinguish or discern good from evil in greater measure and had the courage to choose the good and take responsibility for their actions, would you be pleased with that?

GOD'S WORD SAYS THAT FOR US TO GROW IN THE FAITH, WE ARE TO TRAIN OURSELVES TO DISCERN GOOD FROM EVIL.

Frankly, as the father of three and the grandfather of two, I am thrilled with that sort of discernment in my children. I can apply that definition to any area of their lives, whether it's finances, marriage, the manner in which they are dating, the courses they take at school, the decisions they make about what to watch or what to listen to. When, through their constant use of scriptural teaching and training and the power of the Holy Spirit, they discern in greater measure right from wrong, show a greater level of courage to stand firm and strong, do the right thing, and take responsibility for those decisions, it just doesn't get much better than that.

We can truly see the difference between our children and that man of forty-plus years who fell on his face at the front of the church sanctuary and accepted Jesus Christ. By separating adulthood and maturity, it's easy now to say that he may be an older adult in terms of age, but my sons and my daughter, who are younger in years, have greater spiritual maturity.

SPIRITUAL MATURITY IS REACHED WHEN, THROUGH CONSTANT USE OF SCRIPTURAL TEACHING AND TRAINING AND THE POWER OF THE HOLY SPIRIT, A PERSON DISCERNS GOOD FROM EVIL AND HAS THE COURAGE TO ACT ON THE GOOD AND TAKE RESPONSIBILITY FOR HIS OR HER DECISION.

This then becomes the real objective for us, doesn't it? I can honestly say to a thirteen-year-old, "You are an adult. I believe that with all of my heart. Our responsibility as a church and a family and as your parents is to help you become more spiritually mature. It's not going to happen overnight, and it's not going to happen in every area all at once, but as a parent and a member of this church, I want to help you grow in spiritual maturity each day."

Is that goal reachable? You bet it is. We can look at our lives, the lives of young people, and the lives of older Christians—whether they are babies in their faith or more mature—and agree we are not at the point we want to be; we haven't reached our final resting place. I hope to be better tomorrow than I am today. By defining spiritual maturity in this manner, we see that it is actually attainable.

I want you to think about our sons and daughters again in light of this new definition. I believe if you're honest, you'll see what I've seen in every church where I've conducted rites of passage. You are going to see areas in your children's lives where they're making good decisions. You'll see that in many ways, they're already mature. Like us, they also have areas to work on.

The issue now focuses on the phrase "constant use and training." What does that really look like? I suggest it looks different for a child than for an adult. If we see our young people as adults at age thirteen or fourteen and older, then we're required to treat them differently. Everything we know about their medical, biological, cognitive, and psychological development tells us that typically at thirteen, God has changed their lives. In addition to a physical change, there are emotional and intellectual changes as well. God has, in reality, made them capable of becoming spiritually mature by making them adults.

## A Genuine Testimony

Before I went into the sanctuary to speak at a particular church, a woman approached me and said she felt overwhelmed. She said the issues of sex, maturity, and adulthood were beyond where she and her husband wanted to be with their thirteen-year-old daughter, whom they had tried to protect. I immediately asked her if she and her husband were trying to protect their daughter or themselves. I suggested she go in, listen to the rites-of-passage seminar, and ask God to reveal the truth to her.

Afterward as she was walking out with one of the other mothers, she looked at me tearfully and tried to look away again as if she knew she had been caught. She turned, though, came up to me, and quietly said, "It's so simple, isn't it, when you do it God's way?"

I replied, "I don't know what you mean. Please tell me what you're talking about."

Through her tears, she smiled and said, "Adulthood, maturity. When you understand it God's way, it's very simple, isn't it?"

Again I asked, "What do you mean?"

"You are not going to make this easy for me, are you?"

"I would if I could, but tell me exactly what you mean."

She answered, "My daughter is a young woman, isn't she?"

I responded by asking her if she was making a statement or asking a question.

"I am making a statement. My daughter is a young woman; I just haven't seen it. Chuck, I can't tell you the number of times in the last few months I've looked at my daughter and said, 'Because I am the adult and you are not—that's why.'"

Still crying, she declared, "That ends tonight. My daughter is an adult. I want to help her become more mature."

## FOR PERSONAL REFLECTION OR GROUP DISCUSSION

1. How would you describe the difference between adulthood and maturity?

2. In what ways have parents and the church communicated that maturity is a requirement for adulthood?

3. Read Hebrews 5:13–14. State in your own words what this passage says regarding maturity.

4. Since adulthood and maturity are separated by God as two distinctly different issues, where should parents and churches focus their energy?

5. In what ways can parents impact their children's adulthood and maturity?

6. How will you communicate these definitions and principles to your children?

## CHAPTER 10

# YOU CALL THIS A FAMILY?

One of my favorite movie scenes appears in *Crocodile Dundee*. It's a short sequence that takes place underneath a New York City viaduct. Mick Dundee is walking with his girlfriend, when they are approached by three young men. As they get close to one another, one of the would-be assailants pulls out a knife and tells Mick to give him his wallet. Even Mick's girlfriend, not wanting any harm to come to them, tries to convince Mick to give them his wallet. She appeals to him with what she evidently thinks he can't see with his own eyes: "He's got a knife, Mick!"

Mick reaches into his jacket, pulls out a knife of gargantuan proportions, and then states, "Knife, knife—that's not a knife. This is a knife!" In that moment everyone realizes that by comparison, what the young thug held could not be considered a knife; Mick held the real knife.

I often think of that movie sequence as I go into churches and talk to pastors. The term "church family" is used frequently. I listen to pastors explain how many generations are represented in their church. Some point with great pride toward the section of their sanctuary where all the youth sit together during Sunday morning services. After I have heard the term "church family" so many times, I feel like pulling out a photograph of my mother, surrounded by four generations and holding one of her great-grandchildren on her lap, and saying, "Most churches are not families—this is a family."

## A Real Family

*Family* can be defined as "generations woven together with intentionality." We touch one another, help one another, cry with one another, lift each other up. We stand together through the good times and the bad. We witness the birth of new family members and come together to bury others.

The church today comes together often with multiple generations at the same gathering, but there are very few, if any, intergenerational relationships.

In my family, when just our grandchildren get together, it is not a family gathering. In the same way, church family gatherings or events should include all the generations.

A few months ago, our five-year-old granddaughter, Hannah, came to visit. After some apparently deep thinking, she said to my wife, "You know, Grandma, we need more family dinners. We haven't had very many lately." She and Grandma discussed who would be at such a dinner: Hannah, her sister, her mom and dad, her aunts and uncles, and of course her grandparents. Having made her convincing argument and hearing Grandma acknowledge that we, indeed, needed more family dinners since we hadn't had enough lately, Hannah—now quite satisfied—turned to walk away. Then, to close the deal, she simply looked over her shoulder and said to Grandma, "And I think we need to have lasagna."

## Together ... But Separate

It appears that our churches have become content with generational gatherings minus the interaction of the generations. We have our children's church and departments for junior high, senior high, college and singles, young marrieds, and seniors; and then on Sunday morning we come together for a common worship service in the same room—often still sitting in our separate groups.

I remember going through this as a family when my sons were in middle school or junior high. One Sunday as we entered the church building, they stated that the youth group was all going to sit together during the service. Have you ever felt that something wasn't exactly right, but yet a decision had already been made? I had that feeling,

YOU CALL THIS A FAMILY?

although quite frankly I wasn't sure what I felt to be wrong with the situation.

It only took a few weeks before Billie and I realized what was wrong and instructed our sons that they would sit with us—that Sunday was family time. Our sons quickly pointed out that some of their friends didn't have family there, and our boys felt they should sit with those friends. We merely told our sons to invite their friends to sit with us and become part of our family.

I'm not sure why we take so much pride in our young people sitting together in a group apart from their families. I'm certainly not saying they're doing something wrong. I'm sure every now and then a note is passed back and forth, but that happens all over the sanctuary. After reflecting on this, I've asked several pastors who have thought it is so wonderful to have their youth seated together how happy they'd be if the men came back from an annual event and decided that from that Sunday on, all the men of the church would sit together, and the women and children could sit someplace else. Would they be just as thrilled? I have yet to find a pastor who liked that scenario. Yet we continue to view separation from our own children in the church today as natural.

One of the reasons I believe the church is losing its effectiveness today is because we've stratified the generations. We do our best to keep each of them away from the others. We do it in the name of ministry—to meet people's special needs and make them feel comfortable. In our churches today, we have marginalized people. Often, when kids get into trouble, the first blame is placed on the youth ministry. Though our churches are filled with incredible grandparents and other older adults, the kids who need their influence the most don't get the opportunity to know them.

I'VE ASKED SEVERAL PASTORS HOW HAPPY THEY'D BE IF THE MEN CAME BACK FROM AN ANNUAL EVENT AND DECIDED THAT FROM THAT SUNDAY ON, ALL THE MEN OF THE CHURCH WOULD SIT TOGETHER, AND THE WOMEN AND CHILDREN COULD SIT SOMEPLACE ELSE.

## Parents as "Net Workers"

Now that we have raised the problem, what is the answer and what can we do about it? As parents, we must deliberately foster and encourage intergenerational relationships for our own children. That means we have to look for ways to encourage relationships with folks outside our children's own generational line. I believe we need to be "net workers" on behalf of our children. "Net workers" are the people in our lives who work the safety nets that keep us from falling. One of the great strengths I see in all three of my children is their personal relationships with men and women of all generations. It took me longer to catch on to this than it should have, but fortunately when my children were relatively young, I saw their need for affirmation, acceptance, and encouragement from men and women of all ages.

ONE OF THE GREAT STRENGTHS I SEE IN ALL THREE OF MY CHILDREN IS THEIR PERSONAL RELATIONSHIPS WITH MEN AND WOMEN OF ALL GENERATIONS.

One of my responsibilities as a dad is to deliberately bring my children's lives into close proximity with men and women of all generations and allow them to develop their own relationships. I cannot be with my kids at all times, and I need the help of others to tend their safety nets. It goes beyond just introducing my daughter and sons to my friends. It means encouraging and allowing them to develop their own friendships with those people.

## Keep Rites of Passage Intergenerational

One of the most remarkable things that happens during a rite of passage is when the church—comprised of all generations—comes together to affirm each of the young men and women who are being ceremonially accepted as young adults. When that doesn't happen, though, the young people may reject that which the parents sought to impart in their children's lives.

A friend of mine conducted a rite of passage for his son. Unfortunately, the church family as a whole was not aware of it. A tragedy occurred several months later when a new men's ministry leader was selected. As a sign of support, the senior pastor asked all the men of the church to stand. Without hesitation my friend's son stood, only to find himself being questioned by the men standing and even by his peers who had not stood up. Finally, after hearing enough questions about why he was standing, he simply stated loud enough for those around him to hear, "My dad says I'm a man, and I believe him; so I'm standing."

The rites of passage for our sons and daughters, whether conducted in a church setting or as part of a family gathering, must include a representation of the church family.

Few stories touch my heart as much as that of a young man who was being raised without a father. It was all his mother could do to get him to church with her every Sunday morning. The guys in the "hood" pressured him about being a mama's boy and going to church. After conducting a rite of passage, the church witnessed one of the most remarkable transformations it had ever seen. The young man who had struggled against going with his mother to church once a week now not only went to church but served there. Over a weekend, he went from going to his mother's church to attending *his* church, where he was one of the men.

Sometime later, as the story was related to me, he was approached on the street by some guys from his neighborhood. They began calling him a mama's boy, but the conversation soon centered on acting like a man. At that moment, with incredible clarity and conviction, the young man asked the others, "Do you want to be treated like a man?" When their obvious response was yes, he smiled and said to them, "If you want to be treated like a man, you need to come with me to my church on Sunday."

One of the dreams I have, particularly for our young people, is that anytime they are in a group of people where the subject of family is discussed, they could simply say, "If you want to see a family, you need to come with me to my church on Sunday."

"IF YOU WANT TO BE TREATED LIKE A MAN, YOU NEED TO COME WITH ME TO MY CHURCH ON SUNDAY."

# FOR PERSONAL REFLECTION OR GROUP DISCUSSION

1. How do you think God defines a family?

2. Do the youth of your church sit together, apart from their parents? How do you feel when you think about that? How would you feel if the men or the women of the church no longer sat with their families?

3. How would you characterize the difference between a typical church with multiple generations and one that is intergenerational?

4. What does it mean to you as a parent to be a "net worker" for your children?

5. In what ways can you see yourself increasing your effectiveness as a "net worker" for your children?

# You Cannot Finish
# What You Do Not Start

No two race cars are exactly the same. Body designs differ. Engine tuning differs. Even the philosophy and personalities of the owner, driver, builders, mechanics, and pit crews differ.

Other variables exist, from where you position your car on the track to the number of pit stops you make, tires you use, and adjustments you make to the engine during the race. Despite the variables, however, two undeniable facts exist about racing: One, you must begin at the starting line with everyone else; and two, you must cross the finish line. These are the two absolutes.

It's similar with our children. There are many ways to get them to the starting line; after beginning, there are many ways to run the race. One thing, however, is indisputable: If we want them to cross the finish line, we have to get them to the starting line. Can you imagine a race where the drivers are told at the beginning of the race, "Just start anywhere you want to on the field. You can be in the stadium or out of the stadium; it doesn't really matter. You can be in the track area or out of the track area; it doesn't really matter. If you want to start from a moving position or if you want to start in your pit area, it doesn't really matter. Just start wherever and however it feels best to you at the time."

## The Starting Line: Rites of Passage

Though we'd never permit such a thing in a car race, which has no eternal implications, we permit our kids to start their race to adulthood in that manner. One of the primary purposes of the rite of passage into adulthood is to give parents, children, and churches a clear starting line for the journey called "adulthood and spiritual maturity."

Imagine a father telling his son, "Tomorrow is going to be a great day, son. I've signed you up for a race." The thrilled son asks his dad two questions: "When does it start?" and "Where do I need to be?" Then imagine the dad responding to his son, "Oh, you have to figure that out on your own. You don't need my help. I'll just let you know if you go wrong."

ONE OF THE PRIMARY PURPOSES OF THE RITE OF PASSAGE INTO ADULTHOOD IS TO GIVE PARENTS, CHILDREN, AND CHURCHES A CLEAR STARTING LINE FOR THE JOURNEY CALLED "ADULTHOOD AND SPIRITUAL MATURITY."

Does that sound silly? Of course! Yet how different is that from how we start our young people into adulthood?

Ask most young people, and they'll tell you they're ready to be adults, but they're confused by the conflicting definitions of adulthood they get from their parents, their church, and society. As young people enter into puberty and adulthood, they know they're different and suspect they should be responding to life differently. Therefore they seek answers from the peers racing with them. They assume that if enough of them get together, they can establish their own starting line, determine the rules of the race, and consequently establish their own finish line.

The intentional rite of passage into adulthood that I advocate is, of course, the starting line—not the finish line. However, in far too many cases, the hurdles and requirements placed before the starting line are worse than the race itself. I understand that for the bar mitzvah, bat mitzvah, and other cultural rites of passage there are associated requirements—levels of learning, performance on the part of the individual, challenges to be met. That is all well and good in a society where young people grow up knowing what the challenges and expectations are. Unfortunately, in our westernized American culture, one of the greatest voids is a clearly defined starting line for entry into adulthood. That line moves on a whim. In many ways, adulthood is given and taken away on an almost daily basis.

As we pointed out earlier, when adulthood is associated with the things of this world, it becomes more like a carrot on a stick to be given and taken away. We've discussed how individuals can be regarded as juveniles, children, or adolescents in one area and considered adults—at least on a temporary basis—when it meets the needs and approval of the rest of the adult community.

## A Critical Need

Never has the need for concrete rites of passage into adulthood been as critical in our churches and families as it is today. When we define adulthood and maturity, life begins to make a lot more sense. God's concepts for adulthood and maturity are teachable and reachable.

The harsh reality of the situation is that it appears we've reversed God's plans. If we believe God is the only Creator and he is fully responsible for changing his children's bodies from a childlike body to an adult body, we have to acknowledge that the Creator is also the author of adulthood. Step one in God's plan is that he and he alone will transform our children into adults.

Now we get to the issue of maturity. God's Word tells us to go and make disciples, to train them up, and to help them become mature. God will make the children he's entrusted to us into adults; and we, their families and churches, are to help them become mature. We've had that backward. We've said, "God, when you make our kids mature to our satisfaction, we'll decide when they become adults."

## Extra Baggage

The other key to the starting line is relatively simple but still must be understood. If we acknowledge that God is the Creator and that he alone transforms a person into an adult by changing the body, why do we add our own requirements for adulthood? It's the same as telling our kids they may be adults by God's standards, but our standards are a little higher than God's. In reality, the starting line has been established by God. We move the starting line to suit our purposes—our youth don't measure up; they are not mature enough; they are not making the right decisions; they are not dressing properly or speaking properly. It is as if we are standing between God and our young people.

I've had people in ministry tell me that until young people can meet the requirements and standards for their church, they don't have to be accepted as adults. Young people are going to become adults at some point whether or not they know any Scripture or the doctrinal beliefs of any local church. Even if every single one of our requirements goes unmet, at some point these kids are still going to be adults. Have we not made requirements and privileges for membership more important than recognizing adulthood?

## Make the Starting Line Accessible

One pastor explained to me that for several years they had been conducting a rite of passage on a canoe trip. There were certain things the boys had to do, some involving their fathers, and at the end of that experience they would be considered men. It was a suitable ceremony. I asked the pastor if any young men (or boys, as he would call them) had been unable to attend the trip because of an absent father or a father who had to work. The question was, did he have any young men of the appropriate age who were not able to go on the canoe trip?

YOUNG PEOPLE ARE GOING TO BECOME ADULTS AT SOME POINT WHETHER OR NOT THEY KNOW ANY SCRIPTURE OR THE DOCTRINAL BELIEFS OF ANY LOCAL CHURCH.

The pastor responded affirmatively; several individuals came to mind. So I asked him, "If a boy in your church is not able to go on the canoe trip to become a man, is there any other way for him to become a man in your church—or does he have to go to another church or a gang to become a man?" As the pastor pondered that question, I followed it up with a second: "Since you don't do any rites of passage for your young women, I assume they stay young girls forever—or do they have to leave your church to become women?"

I am not against canoe trips for young men and similar activities for young women. But I am suggesting that this story is one example of a church moving the starting line. I strongly suggested to that congregation that they conduct a universal rite of passage for their young men and their young women for which there were no requirements to meet, no obstacles to overcome—simply show up as a church and let us recognize and accept what God has already done. Then when the young men and their dads and others go on a canoe trip, the issue of manhood has been settled. Now we are talking about helping them grow in spiritual maturity. We have got to get fixed in our minds that what we are celebrating with the rites of passage into adulthood is simply adulthood. Let's not put more into it than we need to, such as requirements that may eliminate some even before they get to the starting line.

## Good Grief!

When I think about the requirements for adulthood, I have to laugh as I compare this to the *Peanuts* cartoon where Lucy is holding the football for Charlie Brown to kick. Every time he runs up to kick the football, Lucy promises to hold it steady, and each time she pulls it back at the last second. His leg whiffs at the air, and he finds himself lying on his back wondering why he believed Lucy one more time. Yet, given the opportunity, he tries it again.

Without rites of passage based on God's plan, the church and Christian parents become Lucy. Our children who have reached puberty know they're different. While they may not use the word *adult* because they think it wouldn't be accepted and we'd laugh at them, they are much like Charlie Brown. Each time we place a ball for them to kick each time we add a requirement for adulthood, they desperately want to succeed and will often, like Charlie, try again to kick the football—only to find that we've moved the ball.

The answer is a simple one, perhaps so simple that it has escaped us for all of these years. The rite of passage into adulthood is the starting line and should be a constant. It should be easy for us to see, and it should provide a common starting point for all.

When we celebrate a rite of passage, it is for young boys and girls together at age thirteen and up. Thirteen, you say? Yes, thirteen. When God changes the body and makes it capable of reproducing life, God himself has transformed the young person into an adult.

The starting line is evident. The question, then, is, do we stay with God's plan or do we rewrite it to satisfy our own desires? The decision is whether to continue with an upside-down plan or to come into agreement with God's plan, in which we would say, "Yes, Lord, these young people are adults, and we accept the responsibility as parents and churches to help them become more mature. Thank you, Lord, for giving us this privilege."

## FOR PERSONAL REFLECTION OR GROUP DISCUSSION

1. What, if anything, did your parents or church do to help launch you into adulthood?

2. Have you had any personal experiences with Christian rites of passage into adulthood? What are your feelings regarding these types of ceremonies?

3. If God is the Creator of life and the Creator of adulthood, what additional requirements are appropriate for parents and churches to place on children before they can be considered adults?

4. In what ways have our requirements and conditions for adulthood become greater than God's?

5. Do you feel that the lack of Christian rites of passage into adulthood has contributed to our children's loss of faith?

# PART

## 3

# CAN ANYONE TELL ME HOW TO GET THERE?

## CHAPTER 12

# RAISING MEN OF HONOR AND WOMEN OF VIRTUE

So what's the big deal about adulthood? We all made it, didn't we? It was seamless and painless. If there was ever a moment in which we questioned our identity or what we were becoming, the support structures of our churches and families were absolutely perfect, and every question about adulthood was answered before we got there. How difficult was that?

Every time I say these words in a church to a group of parents, the audience looks at me like I'm from a different planet. For most of us, the journey to adulthood was confusing, painful, and completely without form or definition. Frankly, most of us were pretty much on our own in that journey. It wasn't because our parents and others didn't love us and believe in us. For most of us, it was simply a matter of silence. No one sat us down and told us what it meant to be an adult.

## Where Are We Headed?

I believe our job is to raise "men of honor" and "women of virtue"— spiritually maturing Christian young adults who are part of a Christian family.

The words *honor* and *virtue* capture the essence of a life that glorifies God. God gives honor to those who follow Christ. Jesus said, "Whoever serves me must follow me; and where I am, my servant also will be. My Father will honor the one who serves me" (John 12:26).

I'm not hung up on specific wording, but I think we need to be able to state our goal in words our children can understand. The term "men of honor" carries with it connotations of safety and security for others, as does the term "women of virtue." Any woman should feel totally safe and secure in the presence of a man of honor. In the same way, men will also feel totally secure in the presence of a woman of virtue, because he doesn't need to protect himself from her.

We need to have a vision for what God desires for our children. By now we realize God is calling on parents to do more than just raise good kids. In reality, God is calling us to disciple those children. Before we get into steps we can take to help raise our kids to keep the faith, I want to throw in one more twist concerning why there is such a battle raging against our children.

## One Creator—God

We're going to delve into some pretty deep theology here. Let me give it to you in a nutshell: There is one Creator—and he is God! All our churches would agree with this statement, yet in reality we give Satan credit for being able to create things. I regularly hear people say that if something is bad in the world, Satan created it that way. But Satan didn't create drugs, alcohol, or ice-covered highways that cause accidents. We cannot have it both ways. Either there is one Creator or there are multiple creators. If there are many who can create, then we would be forced into believing in several gods. Let's go back to the basics. Satan doesn't have the capability to create anything. There is only one Creator, and he is God.

In addition to being the only Creator, God is the only source of truth. And beyond that, God *is* truth. That means if something has been created, God created it. If something is true, it has its source in God. If it is not true, it didn't come from God. We cannot have any doubts about these realities.

## Satan's D3 Strategy

As a result of the facts that Satan cannot create anything and that he certainly is not the source of truth, he has only one alternative: what I call D3 (D to the third power). Satan's only alternative is to take a creation or truth of God and *distort it to deceive us to destroy us*. Grasping this principle is like taking off tinted glasses. We see Satan for who he is and begin to understand how he works.

Satan tries to prevent us from seeing anything the way God intended it—whether that's God's creation or his truth. But as children of God, it is in our nature to know that truth. God has spoken to believers through the apostle John: "You have an anointing from the Holy One, and all of you know the truth. I do not write to you because you do not know the truth, but because you do know it and because no lie comes from the truth" (1 John 2:20–21). Having been created in God's image and regenerated by the Holy Spirit, when righteousness or truth is presented to us it is in our nature to know it. The issue for us as believers, then, is not so much determining *what* is true—but deciding whether we will *obey* the truth.

## The Strategy of Distortion

Christians don't disagree about God's truth. We know his truth. But we most definitely squirm against the truths we don't like. Satan's first strategy, therefore, is to *distort* the truth.

It's like those funny carnival mirrors. They give us a false reflection—one that distorts the truth. It doesn't matter how long you stand in front of those curvy mirrors, the reflection can't change who you are. You are still a creation of God, and no matter how short, tall, fat, or skinny the mirror makes you look, that truth doesn't change. Look at the mirror long enough, though, and you may begin to wonder.

If all you'd ever had as a reference point was a curvy, distorted mirror, what would you assume you looked like? You'd probably believe the lie you saw in the mirror.

## The Strategy of Deception

Satan's purpose for distorting truth is to *deceive* us. His only opportunity to lead us down a path of destruction is to deceive us about what is true so that we will follow a lie.

Many verses in the Bible warn us about being deceived. For instance, in 2 Thessalonians 2:9–10 the apostle Paul wrote, "The coming of the lawless one will be in accordance with the work of Satan

I OFTEN ASK YOUNG FOLKS AND THEIR PARENTS IF THEY HAVE FRIENDS WHO LEFT CHURCH AND THEIR RELATIONSHIP WITH GOD BECAUSE OF A MISUSE OF DRUGS, SEX, OR MONEY.

displayed in all kinds of counterfeit miracles, signs and wonders, and in every sort of evil that deceives those who are perishing. They perish because they refused to love the truth and so be saved."

## The Strategy of Destruction

Finally, the third D represents *destruction*—which is exactly where Satan wants to take us. God's Word tells us, "Your enemy the devil prowls around like a roaring lion looking for someone to devour" (1 Peter 5:8).

It's not hard to find examples of Satan's deception throughout our lives where his undeniable intent is to destroy us. God gave us an astounding array of plant life, some of which Satan has distorted into illicit drugs. God gave us the beautiful gift of sex to be enjoyed in the intimacy of a covenant relationship between a man and woman. Satan's distortion of that gift has destroyed many lives.

Money is another example. We can see that God doesn't consider money inherently evil. Jesus said, "Give to Caesar what is Caesar's, and to God what is God's" (Matt. 22:21). But God led Paul to write,

THE FIRST STEP IN RAISING OUR KIDS TO KEEP THEIR FAITH IS TO BE FULLY WILLING TO EMBRACE GOD'S PLAN AND SET OUR OWN ASIDE.

"People who want to get rich fall into temptation and a trap and into many foolish and harmful desires that plunge men into ruin and destruction. For *the love of money* is a root of all kinds of evil" (1 Tim. 6:9–10). Satan distorts the purpose of money by leading people to define their identity and worth through it.

When I'm speaking in churches, I often ask young folks and their parents if they have friends who left church and their relationship with God because of a misuse of drugs, sex, or money. I have yet to be in a group where no one raises a hand to acknowledge a friend who has fallen prey to Satan's D[3] plan to distort, deceive, and destroy.

## Satan's Strategy for Our Children

There is nothing new or different in Satan's plan of attack where godly adulthood is concerned. Satan's plan is to distort the truth about what constitutes adulthood so that parents and churches do not see the truth with God's eyes. Satan does so to deceive us and, ultimately, destroy the lives of our children before they can enter into the fullness of godly adulthood. More than ever before it is time for parents to say *enough is enough!*

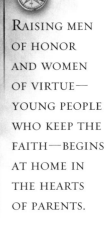

RAISING MEN OF HONOR AND WOMEN OF VIRTUE— YOUNG PEOPLE WHO KEEP THE FAITH—BEGINS AT HOME IN THE HEARTS OF PARENTS.

The first step in raising our kids to keep their faith is to be fully willing to embrace God's plan and set our own aside. We have to see adulthood as a God issue rather than a human issue. We must accept our parental responsibility for the training that leads to spiritual maturity. Instead, we reverse God's plan and expect him somehow to make our kids spiritually mature and let us decide when they are adults.

Through the years that we have been conducting rites of passage, it's been fun to see parents arrive at their "Aha!" moments—moments of awakening. One parent told me, "I have felt these things for several years and have not known how to talk to my children about them. Now I know the words to use, and we are going to sit down and talk." Raising men of honor and women of virtue—young people who keep the faith—begins at home in the hearts of parents. Parents, we have got to get this right before we can pass it on to our children. We have to do more than just hear the message; we have to own it and believe it is from God.

## Four Questions

In the following chapters I'll share some basic principles you can discuss with your own children—either in the context of your local church or just within your family—to launch them with an adult faith of their own. Through a series of four questions, I want to help facilitate discussion between you and your child that will help you get to the starting line of adulthood and on the journey to spiritual maturity:

- Are you ready?

- Are you able?

- Are you prepared?

- Are you willing?

Let the journey begin. Prepare yourself as you turn the page, because the first question is for both you and your child: Are you ready?

## FOR PERSONAL REFLECTION OR GROUP DISCUSSION

1. What does it mean to you to know that God is the Creator of all things and the only source of truth?

2. Can you see Satan's pattern of D³ (distort, deceive, and destroy) at work in our lives today? If so, how?

3. What word pictures come to mind when you hear or read the terms "men of honor" and "women of virtue"?

4. What is the significance of the concept that a child's faith is the faith of his or her parents and an adult's faith is a faith of his or her own?

5. Do you desire to provide a clear pathway for discussion and discovery for you and your children that will recognize them as adults and enable them to find and keep their own faith?

## CHAPTER 13

# ARE YOU READY?

I am told that lawyers are taught never to ask a question to which they don't already know the answer. In this case, before you ask your children if they are ready to hear God's plan for adulthood, you must understand the difference between God's plan and Satan's. This is one of those questions where you personally have to own the answer before you ask the question.

Before asking your kids if they are ready to understand the difference between God's plan and Satan's plan, ask yourself this question one more time: Have I come to accept the fact that God makes our children adults, and our responsibility is to help them on the pathway to spiritual maturity?

If you don't yet understand that truth, don't ask your children if they are ready to hear God's plan for adulthood—because they will see the answer in your eyes before you can finish the question. If God has revealed to you that he and he alone creates an adult and that our job as parents and as a community of believers is to help them on the journey to spiritual maturity, then not only are you able to continue, you feel required to do so. You have no choice. You know what your children need to help them keep their faith. The responsibility falls on you. The question is, are you ready to understand adulthood from God's perspective instead of Satan's?

## Reviewing the Basics: One God; Satan's D3 Strategy

When walking our children through this transition from childhood to adulthood, we must teach them what we've learned—that there is just one Creator, and no one else had a hand in their creation. The reason that adulthood has been so confusing is because, quite frankly, it was confusing for us; as parents, we are still learning. There is nothing wrong with admitting our confusion.

We must help our young people understand how Satan works: his plan of distortion, deception, and destruction. One of the best examples of Satan's destructive tactics is in the area of sex. I do not hesitate to tell young people that sex is an incredible gift from our Creator and Father in heaven. But, by his plan, it was designed for a man and a woman in a covenant relationship.

It is imperative that we share Satan's strategy in this area, because for many, sex is viewed as a means or indicator of adulthood. Our children have to know the truth.

They also need to know that the reason the issue of adulthood has been so confusing is because God has such a wonderful plan for their lives—and Satan knows it. Satan's plan is to *distort* the issue of adulthood in order to *deceive* them so he can *destroy* them before they can walk in the fullness of their adult years—specifically, in their spiritual maturity.

## God's Wonderful Purpose

When you read the press clippings about this generation, you get a negative opinion. We have to be the first to confess that those headlines *do not* and *will not* represent who our sons and daughters really are. It's vital to impress upon your son or daughter the fact that God created them with a purpose and has a wonderful plan for their lives.

Through the prophet Jeremiah, God reassured his people concerning his promises to them following a period of discipline: "'For I know the plans I have for you,' declares the LORD, 'plans to prosper you and not to harm you, plans to give you hope and a future'" (Jer. 29:11). He also stated to the prophet Jeremiah himself, "Before I formed you in the womb I knew you, before you were born I set you apart" (Jer. 1:5).

## Our Authority—The Bible

Sometimes our children listen to Scriptures like this and think they are just ancient words out of an old book. If that's the case, it is our responsibility as parents to help make the Bible real in their lives. Can you tell them unequivocally that the Bible is more than a book? Can you share with all your heart that every word is true?

It is helpful, for ourselves and our children, to conclude that either the Bible is all true or it is all a lie. For if the Bible contains one lie, one error, one mistake, how can we be sure that *any* of it is true? It is either true or it is not—and we have to walk in the fullness of that decision. I can't tell you the number of times I have seen the lights come on over that statement, because we rarely consider those implications.

Pause for a minute and ask yourself the following:

- How do I feel about the Bible?

- How have I portrayed the Bible to my children?

- Is it just a bunch of good stories?

- Is it mostly true?

- Is it helpful at times?

- Do I believe the Bible is the infallible and inerrant Word of God?

THE DIFFERENCE BETWEEN GOD'S PLAN FOR OUR CHILDREN AND SATAN'S PLAN IS THAT SATAN WANTS THEM TO BELIEVE THEY GET TO BE AN ADULT IF THEY ENGAGE IN ADULT BEHAVIOR.

If you've chosen to pick and choose what you believe to be true from the Bible, it's doubtful you'll be able to convince your children of the truth of *any* of it.

## Doing vs. Being

The difference between God's plan for our children and Satan's plan is that Satan wants them to believe they get to *be* an adult if they engage in adult behavior. In other words, he wants them to think that drinking alcohol, doing drugs, and having sex will make them adults. God's plan is to teach them that adulthood is not about what they do; it is about who they are—as determined by their Creator.

## Rights vs. Responsibilities

The plan your children follow will determine how they live their lives. Satan will try to get them to focus on their rights and consume themselves with self-interest. God wants to turn their focus away from their rights and toward their responsibilities.

How this looks in practical terms is that in every area where Satan would want them to ask the question, "What are my rights?" God would ask them to consider, "As a godly young man or woman, what are my responsibilities?"

The first step on the journey to adulthood is to choose God's plan over Satan's.

# FOR PERSONAL REFLECTION OR GROUP DISCUSSION

After reading this chapter and considering the study questions, we encourage you to read and discuss the material with your children.

1. How would you describe to your children the difference between God's plan and Satan's plan for adulthood?

2. As you review the chapter, what are the key points you want to make with your kids?

3. How would you explain to your children the difference between "doing" and "being"?

4. How would you explain to your children the difference between "rights" and "responsibilities"?

## CLOSING PRAYER

a. For children thirteen and older: Pray with them and ask God to confirm in both your heart and theirs that they are *ready* to be adults by God's standards. Acknowledge that Satan has deliberately distorted the godly concepts of adulthood from the Creator and that your desire is for your family to agree with God's plan.

b. For children younger than thirteen: Pray with them for understanding of God's principles regarding adulthood and that God will guide them on a pathway to godly adulthood at the appropriate time.

## CHAPTER 14

# ARE YOU ABLE?

The thought of our children entering adulthood on the basis of the physical changes God has brought about in their bodies can cause a doubtful, gnawing feeling in our stomachs. Even when we acknowledge that God has a plan, we still have to accept our role in that plan. Are you able to accept that role?

Society tells us our young people cannot possibly become adults at the age of thirteen, fourteen, or fifteen. They'd tell us that we're setting our children up for failure by pronouncing them adults at that early age. If we agree with society, our actions will speak louder than our words. So we must settle that doubt and make a choice to trust God.

## God's Strength Doesn't Come in Childhood Doses

It's an undeniable fact: God's strength doesn't come in childhood doses. And since Hebrews 13:8 tells us, "Jesus Christ is the same yesterday and today and forever," that means his mercy, grace, love, power, and strength are the same today as they were in Bible times. And that strength is as available to a thirteen-year-old as it is to a thirty- or forty-year-old. The question is, how willing are we to lay aside our own strength and rely instead on God's? The greater our level of maturity, the easier it is to do this.

Frequently, while speaking about rites of passage in a church setting, I call on a young woman and a young man to come up onto the platform with me. I then ask them to arm wrestle. Since I'm careful to choose a strong young man, the young woman inevitably loses. I ask her to try again—but this time to use God's strength. As she tries—and loses, again—I urge her to use her "father's strength." She assumes I mean her heavenly Father, and often she'll become frustrated. When I clarify my meaning, though, by asking, "Is your father here tonight?" she quickly understands what I mean and wastes no time in calling out for her father to join her on the platform.

Believe me, after watching this young man pin his daughter's arm, her earthly father is ready to help her. I always pick a young woman whose father is one of the larger men of the congregation. You should see the face of the young man when this girl's father steps up to assist her! On every occasion, the young woman will automatically step back, thinking her father will do the arm wrestling without her help. But then I direct her to kneel down and clasp hands with the young man, and I have her father put his arm around her arm and his hand around her hand.

Our kids need to know that God has not said he will fight our battles for us; rather, he has said he will give us *his strength* to help us fight our battles. Paul proclaimed, "I can do everything through him who gives me strength" (Phil. 4:13). This verse makes clear that we still have to fight the battle.

Let's think for a moment about God's strength in terms of cough syrup. The instructions for cough syrup direct certain dosages for certain ages. Interestingly enough, anyone over the age of twelve is considered an adult and has the same strength available to him or her as a twenty-year-old or a sixty-year-old. As God has transformed the body and made an adult, there is no difference in the dosage recommended for a thirteen-year-old than for someone much older. Does it sound as though modern medicine is agreeing with God?

We must help our children to realize they have access to God's strength at all times, and he is willing to strengthen them to become the man or woman he created them to be.

## A Journey—Not a Destination

When we communicate that the goal for our children is not perfection but maturity, and that the only expectation we have of them is growth, we will free them up for the journey. And maturity *is* a journey, not a destination. We will never arrive this side of heaven. God's plan is that day by day—whether we're thirteen years old or white-haired grandparents—we learn greater discernment, gain more courage, and accept more of the responsibility for our actions.

I jokingly tell people my wife's prayer is that I will be more mature tomorrow than I am today. I actually don't have a problem with her prayer, because it is my own prayer for myself. I want to hear more clearly from God tomorrow, have greater courage to act on what he tells me, and always take responsibility for my decisions.

## Our Awesome Redemptive Value

One thing we don't talk about enough with our children is their true value—their value as individuals.

I love the old song that says "when he was on the cross, I was on his mind." Jesus Christ died for each of us individually. Our standing with God the Father is based on our individual relationship with him. This is a message our children need to hear.

Max Lucado tells a wonderful story in his book *No Wonder They Call Him the Savior: Experiencing the Truth of the Cross.* One night two thieves broke into a department store. But instead of stealing things, they just swapped the price tags on different items. A five dollar item was now marked for one hundred fifty, and a three hundred dollar item was now marked for ten. Amazingly, the store was open for several hours before anyone noticed that people were paying the wrong prices without even questioning them.

IT SEEMS THAT SATAN HAS COME IN AND MIXED UP THE PRICE TAGS ON THE THINGS OF TRUE VALUE, SUCH AS OUR CHILDREN.

Aren't we living in a society where the price tags have been switched? It seems that Satan has come in and mixed up the price tags on the things of true value, such as our children. We've become accustomed to paying the price Satan has put on our children versus God's price. One person goes to jail for shooting a deer out of season, while another is permitted to legally abort a child who could have actually survived outside the womb. I'm not justifying shooting deer out of season, but this illustration can help us convey to our children that the only price tag that counts is the one God has placed on them. What value has he assigned them? Simply put, their value is the lifeblood of Jesus Christ, God's own Son.

If God could have sacrificed a goat, a lamb, or a dove on our behalf, he would have done so. His Word says we were "redeemed," or "ransomed"—which means God had to make an exchange of equal or greater value. We are told in 1 Peter 1:18–19, "You know that it was not with perishable things such as silver or gold that you were redeemed from the empty way of life handed down to you from your forefathers, but with the precious blood of Christ, a lamb without blemish or defect." In speaking about himself, Jesus said, "The Son of Man did not come to be served, but to serve, and to give his life as a ransom for many" (Matt. 20:28).

The only thing of equal or greater value that God could offer as a sacrifice was the life of his only begotten Son. God sent his Son to die on a cross—for you and me *individually*.

## Are You Able?

God has not asked us to convince our children with a lot of facts. Instead, he's given us a threefold responsibility: We're to teach our children that God's strength is available to them, that our expectation is growth and not perfection, and that they are so valuable to God he sacrificed his Son to redeem them.

Knowing that, let me ask you again: Are you able?

## FOR PERSONAL REFLECTION OR GROUP DISCUSSION

After reading this chapter and considering the study questions, we encourage you to read and discuss the material with your children.

1. As a result of reading this chapter, how has your thinking changed regarding your children's ability to be the men and women God created them to be?

2. As you review the chapter, what are the key points that you want to make with your children?

3. Why is it so difficult for any of us to rely on God's strength instead of our own?

4. How would you explain to your children the journey to spiritual maturity?

## CLOSING PRAYER

a. For children thirteen and older: Pray with them and ask God to confirm in both your heart and theirs that they are *able* to be godly adults by God's standards. Acknowledge how difficult it is to rely on God's strength, and ask God to give them the wisdom and courage to rely on him.

b. For children younger than thirteen: Pray with them for understanding of God's principles regarding adulthood. Also pray that God will guide them on a pathway that will result in them understanding at the appropriate time that they will be able to be the men and women God created them to be.

## CHAPTER 15

# ARE YOU PREPARED?

It's the winning shot in the movie *Hoosiers*. It's the final play to win the game in *Remember the Titans*. It's *Rudy* running onto the field. It's *Seabiscuit* beating the larger and stronger horse. It's the *Miracle* of the 1980 United States Olympic men's hockey team winning the gold. It's that moment of opportunity when a person or a team is not just ready and able—they're prepared.

We've all witnessed situations in which the underdog emerged the victor. Though nine times out of ten the favored team or player would easily best the underdog, on this day, this occasion, that underdog *did* win—for one reason: They were better prepared.

The win wasn't a matter of being prepared in general, but of being prepared for a specific moment, a specific opportunity or challenge. Our children must do the same. It is one thing for us as their parents and their faith community to acknowledge they are *ready* and certainly *able* to be adults. One of our final steps is to make sure they are *prepared* to embark upon the journey before them.

The preparation for the journey requires an understanding of three steps: salvation, connection, and sanctification.

## Salvation

The first question to ask our children is "Do you know Jesus, and does Jesus know you?" It's important for us to understand what is being asked and what is *not* being asked within that question. We're not asking if they know *about* Jesus—that is, can they name the miracles he performed, recite the words he said, or repeat the parables he taught. This is not an issue of the head, but an issue of the heart.

Before you share this question with your children, I want to warn you that we Christians have become almost immune to evangelistic messages—particularly if we've been in the church for any length of time. Many believe that mere attendance at church and a desire to do good puts us in good standing with Jesus.

ASK GOD TO BRING TO REMEMBRANCE THE MOMENT YOU SURRENDERED YOUR LIFE TO HIM AND JESUS CHRIST BECAME YOUR PERSONAL LORD AND SAVIOR.

That certainly is not what the Bible teaches. In fact, in speaking of the day of judgment, Jesus said, "Not everyone who says to me, 'Lord, Lord,' will enter the kingdom of heaven, but only he who does the will of my Father who is in heaven. Many will say to me on that day, 'Lord, Lord, did we not prophesy in your name, and in your name drive out demons and perform many miracles?' Then I will tell them plainly, 'I never knew you. Away from me, you evildoers!'" (Matt. 7:21–23).

The point is made again in the parable of the ten virgins. Five of the virgins had to go buy oil for their lamps and therefore were not prepared for the moment when the bridegroom presented himself, representing Christ's return. When they arrived later with oil in their lamps and said, "Open the door for us!" the bridegroom replied, "I tell you the truth, I don't know you" (Matt. 25:11–12).

If you've never asked the question of yourself, you need to do so before you ask it of your child. Don't answer the question immediately. Pray about it for at least twenty-four hours. Ask God to bring to remembrance the moment you surrendered your life to him and Jesus Christ became your personal Lord and Savior. Pray that God will lovingly show you a blank screen if you actually have never surrendered your life to Jesus. Until confronted with this question, countless men and women—young and old—have told me they thought they were okay because they attended church and tried to be good and do what was right.

Think about it for a moment. "Do you know Jesus, and does Jesus know you?" Will you be able to look at him and say, "I know you"? Do you have every assurance in your heart that he will respond, call you by name, and say, "I know you too"? Parents, first answer these questions for yourself, and then ask them of your child.

## Connection

For some of us the issue of salvation for our children has been settled for some time now. In other cases, the questions in the previous section helped you or your child to settle the issue. Yet even if there is some uncertainty at this point, you must continue and teach them the importance of connecting in fellowship with other believers. In a global sense, they should understand that they are part of the universal church, the bride of Christ. On a local level, they need to plug in to a local congregation where they can build relationships with other believers.

Often, the discussion about committing to a local church body sounds more like a threat than an invitation. Some have been told that if they don't attend church, they may lose their salvation. That's simply not true and not supported by anything in God's Word.

That brings us to a potentially paradoxical situation. If we can't lose our salvation by *not* committing to a church body, why is it imperative we get involved there? Simply put, God tells us we are all one body functioning together. He also tells us that all spiritual gifts have been given for the building up of the body. By using our gifts to complement the gifts of others, we grow stronger together.

We need to warn our children that because they have incredible value and potential, Satan is going to try to pull them out of church. Let them know they're in a battle. Let them know we're in that battle too. If you drifted from church for a season, share what you learned. Share your regrets. Be honest about the dangers of wandering.

It's possible, at this point, that your children may indicate they're not willing to commit to the church. This doesn't change their adult standing in God's eyes. And it doesn't change the fact that you need to instruct them on the importance of plugging in to a fellowship. Give them the truth and pray that God will change their hearts.

*We* know that walking in the fullness of God's purpose includes active church involvement, but it may take our children longer to accept that truth. We must be patient, and we must *not* hold their adult status hostage until they respond to the church the way we want them to.

> WE [PARENTS] MUST BE PATIENT, AND WE MUST NOT HOLD THEIR [OUR CHILDREN] ADULT STATUS HOSTAGE.

In separate conversations with both of my sons, I explained how much it thrilled me to have our entire family in church together. I told them I realize there might come a day when they won't choose my church to be their church—and as hard as that might seem, I would be okay with it. The important thing is for them to have a faith community or local church that they are part of because of who they are, not because it's Mom and Dad's church. It's a hard thing for a parent to think about, let alone to do, but I encourage you to allow your children, as adults, to find their own church at the appropriate time. For our sons, that talk took place in their senior year of high school.

Youth groups are not the same thing as church. The fact that your son or daughter may attend a youth group at another church doesn't mean they call that their church home. At one point in time our sons attended several different youth groups each week—but they called our church "home."

> NO ONE IS BETTER EQUIPPED THAN PARENTS TO HELP THEIR CHILDREN LOOK FOR A CHURCH HOME.

At the appropriate time, help your children find a church where their faith can be real to them. Again, I'm not suggesting that this is at age thirteen or fourteen. Perhaps the earliest age I would consider would be seventeen or eighteen.

No one is better equipped than parents to help their children look for a church home. I would also add that giving your child the choice about churches doesn't mean they will even want to leave. If we create the proper environment in our churches, our children will typically find our church the safest and healthiest place to be.

## Sanctification

The final issue of preparedness concerns the subject of sanctification. The word *sanctified* means "set apart." For purposes of our discussion, I want to specifically address an area of sanctification that falls under the topic of "purity." We have allowed society to confuse the issue of purity with virginity.

Some parents go into an immediate tailspin when this topic is broached. Let me assure you that your kids do not expect you to be perfect. By now we have dispelled any thoughts of that. More than anything, they simply want us to be truthful with them.

This is not intended to be a "true confession" time between you and your kids. Frankly, I'm not comfortable suggesting we reveal all our mistakes to thirteen-year-olds. Nor do I think it is entirely healthy. But as our sons have grown older, I have shared more about my past in a manner that is both honest and positive.

YOUR KIDS DO NOT EXPECT YOU TO BE PERFECT. BY NOW WE HAVE DISPELLED ANY THOUGHTS OF THAT.

There are some absolute truths about purity that we must embrace before conveying them to our children. Let's begin by acknowledging one lie that permeates our society and attacks our children: that the only thing we have to be concerned about is a technical or literal concept of virginity. Allowing our children to believe they can do anything they want to do up to the act of intercourse throws open the doors to promiscuity and defilement. Purity is not the same thing as virginity. Purity from God's perspective encompasses everything we think, hear, see, say, and feel with our hearts. It encompasses the way we touch others and allow others to touch us. I certainly don't want to downplay the importance of speaking directly to the issue of virginity before marriage. But along with contending that God's standards are higher than simply stopping short of intercourse, I want to state that even if virginity has been lost, God still loves our young people and can restore their purity.

It's also important to come against a deadly lie that has corrupted several generations—the lie that there are just some things you can't talk about at home or in church. This relegates some of the critical issues of life to locker rooms and dark alleys. I once heard a person say that everything he knew about being a man he learned in a locker room at a young age. How tragic! We must help our children understand that there is nothing that cannot be talked about in an appropriate way in our homes or even in our churches. I don't necessarily mean this in the context of typical classes or from the pulpit—but in the appropriate setting with men and women of God who are willing to talk to young men and women about the poisons Satan tries to pump into our hearts and minds.

## Responding to God's Call

One of the most remarkable moments during any rites-of-passage weekend is the conclusion of the "R U Prepared?" session, in what we simply refer to as the "purity altar call." We don't spend hours addressing perverse sexual issues or drawing out embarrassing, intimate questions. On behalf of their parents and their pastor, I look the young people in the eyes and tell it to them straight: "The world would have you believe that you can do anything you want to do up to the act of intercourse and still be okay. That is a lie straight from the pit of hell. The truth is that inappropriate kissing, misplaced hands under clothing, fondling, lying, cheating, stealing, dark thoughts, or rebellious hearts don't violate the technical virginity of a person—but all of them break Almighty God's heart because of the loss of your purity."

I tell the young people that the front of the church will be reserved just for them—for the sole purpose of allowing them to bring personal issues to a loving God and ask him for forgiveness and restoration of purity. I also assure them that no one is going to ask them about their reason for going to the altar. I explain to everyone present, including parents, that in a moment like this we can give the young people two choices: We can either force them to discuss the issue with us or allow them to present the issue before God. I also suggest that unless God has put any of us in the business of forgiving sins, restoring purity, and granting eternal life, we should trust God and leave it in his hands as the One who can.

People in many churches have told me they can't possibly imagine any young people stepping forward at the risk of embarrassing themselves. For more than seven years, just the opposite has always been the case. In church after church, young people move without hesitation from where they are seated to the front of the church for the sole purpose of asking God to forgive whatever issue is in their lives and restore the purity they desire. This generation isn't afraid of anything; they just want the truth spoken to them. When they hear the truth, they respond.

"IF YOU DON'T KNOW JESUS, WHAT IS THERE TO KEEP YOURSELF PURE FOR?"

One young woman in a small Baptist church spoke to the entire congregation the following evening: "Until Mr. Stecker spoke to us on the issue of purity, no one had ever mentioned it to me in church before." Then she made a statement I have thought of many times since. "If you don't know Jesus, what is there to keep yourself pure for?" That young woman asked a great question, a question that revealed incredible comprehension.

What an awesome opportunity every parent has to share the truth with their own children! I have believed for a long time that God's principles must be both teachable and reachable. In too many cases in the church today, faith issues are taught but don't honestly appear to be achievable by the young men and women listening. When we make a decision to live in accordance with God's plans, we find his principles both teachable and reachable.

Being prepared is being in a right relationship with Almighty God. It boils down to this question that we as parents must also answer with our children: "Are you prepared?" They can be—if we will just tell them the truth.

## FOR PERSONAL REFLECTION OR GROUP DISCUSSION

After reading this chapter and considering the study questions, we encourage you to read and discuss the material with your children.

1. How would you describe to your children the three areas that they should place before God as they prepare to be received as adults?

2. Read with your kids Matthew 7:21–23 and Matthew 25:1–12. What is the difference between knowing about Jesus and knowing Jesus?

3. Pray with your children that God would show them with the eyes of their hearts the moment they surrendered their lives to Jesus Christ and he became their Lord and Savior.

4. Give your children a few minutes, and then ask them to share what God revealed to them. Be prepared to pray with them if they realize they have never prayed specifically to surrender their lives to Christ.

5. Read with your children 1 Corinthians 12:12–26, and discuss what it means to be a part of the body of Christ.

6. How would you explain to your children the difference between "purity" and "virginity"?

7. Read together 1 Peter 1:22 and 1 John 1:9. Discuss how God purifies all those who sincerely repent and ask for forgiveness.

8. Before you pray with your kids, make sure they understand that they will be given an opportunity to ask God to restore purity in any area of their lives—but that you will not ask them about any details. You must create a safe place for their prayers.

## CLOSING PRAYER

Pray with your children and ask God to reveal to them any area in which they have lost purity. Then invite them to pray and sincerely ask for forgiveness and the restoration of their purity.

## CHAPTER 16

# ARE YOU WILLING?

Many parents get excited just reading the title to this chapter. The question "Are you willing?" would seem to indicate that this is the moment of truth when we as parents get to tell our kids exactly what the requirements are—how clean we expect them to keep their rooms, what kind of grades they should get in school, and what type of clothes they should wear—and then put it all on the line and ask them if they are willing to meet our demands in return for our acceptance of them as adults. If that's what you're thinking, you're going to be a little disappointed.

Hopefully by now we are in agreement that the issue of adulthood should be based on God's plan. I have looked at a number of rites-of-passage programs that require several weeks or even months of studying in advance of the actual ceremony. Steps *do* need to be taken prior to the rites of passage in any program, but we must be certain that any requirements placed before our sons and daughters are part of clear pathways and do not have the potential to become obstacles.

## Six Mile Markers

The concept of "Are you willing?" can best be explained by the point made in chapter 13. We're talking about spiritual maturity, which is a journey—not a destination. Does this mean there are no requirements? Let's take a look at this in a different way. God has certain expectations for each of us. I suggest they are more like mile markers on the highway than legal requirements.

If you understand the mile-marker system in the United States, you can determine if you are going in the right direction. Let's say my intention is to drive from Denver to Kansas City on Interstate 70. On a pitch-black night, place me anywhere in Colorado or Kansas without a light or a reference point in sight, in a vehicle without a compass, spin me around, point me in a direction, and within two miles I could tell you if I was going in the right direction.

Mile markers start in the west and increase to the east or start in the south and increase to the north. After seeing the first mile marker, I would continue to travel in the same direction. If the second mile marker was the next higher number, I would know that I was traveling east in the right direction from Denver to Kansas City. On the other hand, if the subsequent mile marker was the next lower number, I would know immediately that I was traveling west and that I needed to turn around and go the other way. This may not sound very spiritual, but it helps me focus on the markers we can use to let God guide us.

> GOD HAS CERTAIN EXPECTATIONS FOR EACH OF US. I SUGGEST THEY ARE MORE LIKE MILE MARKERS ON THE HIGHWAY THAN LEGAL REQUIREMENTS.

There are six key areas we discuss with young people that are like mile markers—not legal traps that they could fall into and thereby lose their status of adulthood. We have to keep remembering that if God gives adulthood, then only God can take it away. It's not for us to dangle adulthood like a carrot on a stick, offer a little bit, and then pull it back. We also may continually need to reinforce to our children that our expectation is not for them to be at the finish line on any of these areas, but that being an adult means they understand the importance of each of these elements and are willing to embark upon the journey to spiritual maturity.

The following six characteristics help us know if we are traveling in the right direction toward being more spiritually mature and Christlike:

- Purified

- Submitted

- Prepared

- Self-controlled

- Trusting

- Setting an example

These are also the six elements that we use in our ministry in the "covenant of manhood" and "covenant of womanhood" that are provided to each church to be presented and signed by their young adults as part of the rites-of-passage ceremony. As we look at these areas individually, I'll begin each section with the corresponding commitment from these covenants.

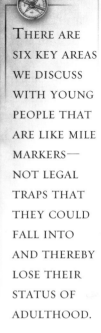

THERE ARE SIX KEY AREAS WE DISCUSS WITH YOUNG PEOPLE THAT ARE LIKE MILE MARKERS— NOT LEGAL TRAPS THAT THEY COULD FALL INTO AND THEREBY LOSE THEIR STATUS OF ADULTHOOD.

## Purified

Covenant commitment: I will purify myself by obeying the truth and acknowledging that Jesus Christ is the way and the truth and the life.

In the previous chapter we talked about the importance of purity. The key point to make with our sons and daughters here is simply this: We live in a dirty world, and it is Satan's desire to use the filth of this world to defile us and destroy our purity. Spiritually maturing young men and women understand they constantly have to maintain their purity.

A couple of points must be kept in mind. First, God has done all he needs to do to maintain our purity. He provided his Son as the sacrificial Lamb to die for our sins. A careful look at key Bible verses on purity shows that the responsibility from that moment forward is on us. Peter wrote, "Now that you have purified yourselves by obeying the truth so that you have sincere love for your brothers, love one another deeply, from the heart" (1 Peter 1:22). Paul charged the Corinthians, "Since we have these promises, dear friends, let us purify ourselves from

COVENANT COMMITMENT: I WILL PURIFY MYSELF BY OBEYING THE TRUTH AND ACKNOWLEDGING THAT JESUS CHRIST IS THE WAY AND THE TRUTH AND THE LIFE.

everything that contaminates body and spirit, perfecting holiness out of reverence for God" (2 Cor. 7:1). Purity, therefore, comes from obeying the truth and confessing our sins—acknowledging the dirt that has attached itself to us.

Godly men and women understand that sometimes our circumstances or environment—over which we have no control—can make us feel dirty and defiled. For example, a young person walking through the halls of his high school, through no fault of his own, happens to hear vile, filthy language coming from two other students. He feels pretty dirty and cringes in his spirit, even though he had no choice in what he heard.

I believe when Satan can't get you to participate on his playing field, his plan is to throw dirt on you from the sidelines. Again, godly young men and women need to understand spiritual maturity and the mile markers, or indicators, that say, "You're going the wrong direction. Turn around, go the other way, and be purified and clean."

## Submitted

Covenant commitment: I will submit myself to every authority instituted among men, acknowledging that all authority comes from God.

COVENANT COMMITMENT: I WILL SUBMIT MYSELF TO EVERY AUTHORITY INSTITUTED AMONG MEN, ACKNOWLEDGING THAT ALL AUTHORITY COMES FROM GOD.

Submission is not an easy area, and, quite frankly, the generation of parents of which I am a part hasn't set a very good example for our children. Yet that doesn't relieve us from the responsibility of understanding God's plan and walking under the authority he's placed over us.

Although certainly not the only verse about submitting to authority, Romans 13:1 is key: "Everyone must submit himself to the governing authorities, for there is no authority except that which God has established. The authorities that exist have been established by God." Hebrews 13:17 states, "Obey your leaders and submit to their authority. They keep watch over you as men who must give an account. Obey them so that their work will be a joy, not a burden, for that would be of no advantage to you." First Peter 2:13–17 tells us we're to submit ourselves "to every authority instituted among men." We see in Romans 13:1 that the authority instituted among men is from God, so that doesn't give us any loopholes.

I believe the significant point for our young people to know is that God is not going to use them in positions of authority, in true God-given authority, until they have themselves been men and women properly submitted to authority. It just makes sense! God doesn't give us an out or an excuse; he simply tells us throughout the Bible to submit to authority.

## Prepared

Covenant commitment: I will prepare my mind for action to serve God as he calls me.

"Prepare your minds for action; be self-controlled; set your hope fully on the grace to be given you when Jesus Christ is revealed" (1 Peter 1:13). "In your hearts set apart Christ as Lord. Always be prepared to give an answer to everyone who asks you to give the reason for the hope that you have. But do this with gentleness and respect" (1 Peter 3:15). "Preach the Word; be prepared in season and out of season; correct, rebuke and encourage—with great patience and careful instruction" (2 Tim. 4:2).

COVENANT COMMITMENT: I WILL PREPARE MY MIND FOR ACTION TO SERVE GOD AS HE CALLS ME.

A clear mark of spiritual maturity can be found in an individual's preparedness to pursue the plans God has for him or her. We can take this another step and also say that our preparedness has a great deal to do with our right relationship with God. The better our relationship, the better prepared we're going to be.

As we understand and truly accept the fact that no one could possibly love us more or have greater plans for us than our Father in heaven, why would we not want to be prepared and help our children be prepared for the very best that God has for them?

## Self-controlled

Covenant commitment: I will be self-controlled in all I do, acknowledging that the "self" who controls me is Jesus Christ who lives in me.

Paul's letter to Titus gives instruction on what is to be taught to the members of the church—both younger and older. Paul specifically stated that the younger men and women should be challenged and encouraged to be self-controlled. (See Titus 2:3–6.) Peter's letters also emphasize self-control. "Prepare your minds for action; be self-controlled" (1 Peter 1:13). "The end of all things is near. Therefore be clear minded and self-controlled so that you can pray" (1 Peter 4:7). "Be self-controlled and alert. Your enemy the devil prowls around like a roaring lion looking for someone to devour" (1 Peter 5:8). "Make every effort to add to your faith goodness; and to goodness, knowledge; and to knowledge, self-control" (2 Peter 1:5–6).

COVENANT COMMITMENT: I WILL BE SELF-CONTROLLED IN ALL I DO, ACKNOWLEDGING THAT THE "SELF" WHO CONTROLS ME IS JESUS CHRIST WHO LIVES IN ME.

We weren't born with self-control, but the Bible tells us we can decide to be self-controlled. I suggest the easiest way to apply this to our lives is to think of "self-controlled" as "Christ-controlled." It's a decision of the will—surrendering my will to God's—that leaves self-control in God's hands.

## Trusting

Covenant commitment: I will bear the pain of any unjust suffering and not retaliate, but entrust my life to him who always judges justly.

I believe the most important thing about the subject of trusting is that it's much easier for our children to trust God if we've shown them they can trust us. It's hard to explain to young people how they can trust in a loving Father when the gateway to that confidence has been a parent who has consistently broken trust with his or her own child.

Many state unequivocally that they love and believe in God, but their lifestyle reveals that they don't seem to trust God to be who he says he is or to do what he says he will do. Spiritually maturing young men and women understand that trusting God is critical to their right relationship with God the Father.

The Bible is full of verses, such as Proverbs 3:5, that tell us to trust the Lord: "Trust in the LORD with all your heart and lean not on your own understanding." As a former military officer, I love Psalm 20:7: "Some trust in chariots and some in horses, but we trust in the name of the LORD our God." Another simple but powerful statement about trust is found in Hebrews 2:13: "I will put my trust in him." God tells us to trust him because he wants more for us than we want for ourselves.

> COVENANT COMMITMENT: I WILL BEAR THE PAIN OF ANY UNJUST SUFFERING AND NOT RETALIATE, BUT ENTRUST MY LIFE TO HIM WHO ALWAYS JUDGES JUSTLY.

There is another part of this concept of trust that we need to understand. Peter wrote this about Jesus: "When they hurled their insults at him, he did not retaliate; when he suffered, he made no threats. Instead, he entrusted himself to him who judges justly" (1 Peter 2:23). The significance of this statement is profound. Bad things are going to happen to good people. Being a Christian doesn't mean everything will be perfect or that we will have no worries or pain. In fact, just the opposite is typically true. Yet we must strengthen our children by teaching them to trust God even when they don't understand why he has allowed trials. When things aren't perfect or when they feel persecuted, the answer is in trusting God—not in retaliation or vengeance.

## Setting an Example

Covenant commitment: I will set an example for other believers in speech, life, love, faith, and purity—in all that I am and in all that I do.

Paul wrote his first letter to Timothy after commissioning Timothy to lead the church at Ephesus. Paul instructed his junior partner, "Don't let anyone look down on you because you are young, but set an example for the believers in speech, in life, in love, in faith and in purity" (1 Tim. 4:12). After washing his disciples' feet at the Last

Supper, Jesus said, "I have set you an example that you should do as I have done for you" (John 13:15).

The greatest influence we can have as Christians is to set the right example. The power of a good example is often underestimated. We have a tendency in the church to focus on large crowds and those who have been called to speak to them. But it's hard to imagine a greater power or force for the kingdom of God than all God's children living out their faith and setting a positive example.

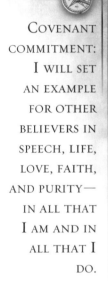

COVENANT COMMITMENT: I WILL SET AN EXAMPLE FOR OTHER BELIEVERS IN SPEECH, LIFE, LOVE, FAITH, AND PURITY— IN ALL THAT I AM AND IN ALL THAT I DO.

Many of our young people have been conditioned to believe they aren't old enough to have a true impact for the kingdom. We have a responsibility to help them realize that their future ministry, while it may be much different, is no more important than the ministry God has for them right now.

The issue of setting a proper example is so important that in 1 Corinthians 8:9–13, God warned us not to be stumbling blocks to those weaker in their faith who might be "destroyed" by our actions. In 2 Corinthians 6:3 Paul reiterated, "We put no stumbling block in anyone's path, so that our ministry will not be discredited."

Lastly, I suggest that parents encourage their sons and daughters by helping them understand that God would never call them to something they weren't equipped for and capable of doing. God wouldn't tell young men and women to set an example for the rest of the church were it not for their incredible capacity to do so. God knows what's inside us when we don't know it ourselves.

So these are the mile markers, the indicators, that indicate whether we are moving down the right path, and each spiritual marker will serve us well all of our lives.

## The Critical Question

The question comes back to "Are you willing?" The question is not "Are you willing to do all of these things perfectly?" or "Have you already done so?" Rather, the question is "Are you willing to acknowledge that these areas of our lives are important to God—and that through discernment in the power of the Holy Spirit he will guide us, showing us whether we are moving in the right direction?"

In churches where we conduct rites-of-passage seminars, the actual ceremony takes place immediately following this session. Whether you use this book for preparation as part of a church-wide effort or with family and friends, it is critical that you convey to your children that none of these six areas is easy. If we are honest, all adults struggle with one or more of these issues. Spiritually maturing men and women are not those who never fail or stumble; they are those who realize they are moving in the wrong direction and make a conscious decision to turn around.

As we ask our sons and daughters if *they* are willing, we must also ask ourselves if *we* are willing—to recognize and accept them as the young men and women whom God has created them to be.

# FOR PERSONAL REFLECTION OR GROUP DISCUSSION

After reading this chapter and considering the study questions, we encourage you to read and discuss the material with your children.

1. In response to the final note of this chapter, are you willing to recognize and accept your children as the young men and women God has created them to be?

2. As you review the chapter, what are the key points you want to make with your children?

3. Review again each of the six covenant commitments, and be sure your kids understand these are mile markers or indicators of spiritual maturity to guide them.

4. Explain to your children that they are to consider each of the points you have discussed and that you will give them time to think about them before you actually bless them as a young men and women.

# CLOSING PRAYER

a. For children thirteen and older: Pray with them and ask God to confirm in both your heart and theirs that they are not just ready, able, and prepared, but also *willing* to be the adults God has created and called them to be.

b. For children younger than thirteen: Pray with them for understanding of God's principles regarding adulthood and that he will guide them on a pathway to godly adulthood at the appropriate time.

## CHAPTER 17

# A FUTURE AND A DESTINY

It had already been an evening like none other at the Crossroads Ministry Centre (or what I affectionately refer to as the "Mighty Church on the Curve") in Tioga, Louisiana. The ceremonial rite of passage was the culmination of a weekend in which the young men and women of the church, along with their families, had discovered the principles of godly adulthood and spiritual maturity. The ceremony itself would leave an indelible mark on the lives of all those present.

The parents of one young man, who had found a home at Crossroads Ministry Centre, came to participate in the event even though they attended a different church. Like many parents, I think they were just happy their son was in a church somewhere. The young man's older brother also came, with a friend, and sat several rows behind his parents. There was a youthful cockiness in his walk and in his speech, and I'm not sure he even knew why he was there—except his parents had told him to come to support his brother.

When it came time for their son's blessing, I watched the parents come forward and place their hands on their kneeling son. The father then began to pray. It was as if the heavens opened up not just to hear his words but to connect with them. No one in the church could move as this father poured out his blessing on his son. Believe me, when he was done, there was no doubt that this young man had been blessed.

I couldn't help but notice a distinctly different demeanor come over the older brother, who was sitting toward the rear of the church. I wasn't sure at the time what it meant.

## Our Father's Blessing

The ceremony continued until all the young people who were participating had come forward and knelt before their parents (or spiritual
parents) to be blessed as a young man or a young woman. Although
it had been a long evening and we were later into the night than we
had anticipated, Pastor Dugas couldn't let the moment go by until he
gave one last invitation. He asked if there were any there who had
never known their earthly fathers' blessing and desired to be prayed
for and blessed at this time. Before the last of his words had left
his mouth, the older brother of the young man I mentioned earlier
leaped from his seat as if he had been shot from a cannon. He ran
forward to where his parents were seated and grabbed his father's
arm, crying out, "Do me, Dad. Please, do me!"

His father was momentarily stunned, but then he got out of his
seat. Seeing that, his son ran to the front of the church and dropped
to his knees to await his parents' prayer and his father's blessing. I
watched these same parents place their hands on their son and bless
him to no less degree than they had their younger son. And again it
was as if the heavens opened up to receive this father's words and
pour out a blessing on his son.

There is incredible power in our fathers' blessings. How is it that
a few words can be so life-changing? I think we were created with a
longing for the affirmation of our fathers.

## The Family Blessing

When I was first taught the concept of "the father's blessing" as a part
of a rite of passage into adulthood (more specifically, manhood, since
I was working only with young men at the time), I had no experience or frame of reference. My ministry background had not been as
a pastor. During the first few rites of passage I led, I felt in my spirit
that something was missing. Eventually I discerned that the missing
component was the complete family—specifically the mothers. If the
mother wasn't included, when and where would she be able to release
her sons and daughters into God's hands and bless them as adults?

I also believe that the Bible, God's inspired Word, specifically tells
us of the need for our fathers' blessing. In chapter 27 of Genesis we

read the account of Isaac giving the blessing of the firstborn to his son Jacob instead of Esau—albeit Jacob and his mother, Rebekah, had tricked Isaac into doing so. In verse 33 Isaac spoke to Esau regarding the blessing he had just bestowed on Jacob: "I blessed him—and indeed he will be blessed!" We also read in Genesis 48 and 49 that Jacob, in his later years, blessed two of his grandsons as his own sons and then blessed his twelve sons—the founders of the twelve tribes of Israel.

God certainly never says that our mothers' blessings don't matter or count. But I believe there is a unique power in our earthly father's blessing; it is different, not superior, to our mother's blessing and prayers. I also believe God calls men to take the lead in the family blessing of our sons and daughters.

> IF THE MOTHER WASN'T INCLUDED, WHEN AND WHERE WOULD SHE BE ABLE TO RELEASE HER SONS AND DAUGHTERS INTO GOD'S HANDS AND BLESS THEM AS ADULTS?

It has been almost twenty years since Gary Smalley and John Trent wrote *The Blessing*. Several other books have been written since then that continue to build on the scriptural foundation Smalley and Trent outlined. Nearly every book I've read uses the same five elements of the blessing that Smalley and Trent identified from the Bible. Here is their definition of a "family blessing":

> A family blessing begins with *meaningful touching*. It continues with a *spoken message of high value*, a message that pictures a *special future* for the individual being blessed, and one that is based on an *active commitment* to see the blessing come to pass.[1]

Smalley and Trent pointed out the critical elements of a family blessing:

- meaningful touch
- a spoken message
- attaching high value to the one being blessed
- picturing a special future for the one being blessed
- an active commitment to fulfill the blessing

Just as we are to bless our children and others in their coming and going, other milestones call for specific blessings.

In his book *The Ancient Paths,* Craig Hill, president of Family Foundations International, identified a minimum of seven times in our lives when we need to be blessed: conception, in utero, birth, infancy, puberty, marriage, and older age.[2] He stated that in the absence of that blessing, there is a great likelihood that a curse will replace it. Don't get hung up on the word *curse,* but think of it in the context of Craig's definitions. He sees a blessing as an opportunity "to empower to prosper," and says a good definition of cursing is "to disempower from prospering."[3]

Think of it like a car: To bless would be the equivalent of filling the tank with gas so the car can function as it was designed; not to bless—or to curse—would be the equivalent of not filling the tank, or in some cases even draining the tank. The blessing on the part of the parents is really the connecting of their son or daughter to the power that comes from God to walk in the fullness of who God created them to be.

## Grabbing the Power Line

Let me give you another illustration. As a child, I spent several summers at my aunt and uncle's farm south of St. Joseph, Missouri. Many of the farms in the area had electric fences. I'm not sure how old I was when I learned this, but the lesson has stayed with me. If you're walking with someone near an electric fence and you grab the hand of that person or touch them and then grab the electric fence with your other hand, the current will go through you and zap the other person. (I'm sure you were never ornery enough to do this, but perhaps you've heard of others who have done it!) You are not the electricity, but you *are* the conduit. I believe it's the same way with the blessing.

I often have this picture in my mind of a power line hanging from heaven with more voltage than we can possibly imagine. God gives parents the privilege of laying our hands on our sons and daughters and, spiritually speaking, reaching toward heaven and grabbing the power line. We are neither the power nor the source of the power, but the power of the blessing allows us to be the conduit so God's power may flow freely to our children. Our families and churches have lost the understanding of the power carried in the blessing. The ancient Hebrews believed the blessing imparted power for living and guided individuals to their future and destiny. They specifically believed the blessing given to a child at the transition point into adulthood was like a doorway a child would pass through. Without that blessing there was no doorway.

Many years ago, Johannes Pedersen wrote insightfully about the Israelites' views:

> The blessing is a mental gift, and as such it has its root in something which partly loses itself in mystery. Behind the blessing of the individual stand the fathers; from them he has derived it, and its strength depends on their power. When all is said and done, it rests in powers which lie behind all human capability. When a man is blessed, it may also be expressed in the way that God is with him.... This expression that Yahweh or God is with one is only another term for the blessing.[4]

(Before I lose any of the mothers reading this, we must be quick to acknowledge that much of the writing regarding the blessing centers on masculine nouns and pronouns. That doesn't mean God loves women any less or that the power of the blessing is less for them.)

## A Future and a Destiny

A key component of the blessing we seem to have lost over the years is the element regarding a young person's future and destiny. Words of blessing have been restricted only to those areas in which the individual performs well. The blessing has become a reward for good behavior, for behavior that's pleasing or acceptable to us.

This is not God's plan. In fact, withholding the blessing from our children creates a greater tendency for them to spiral downward. Regardless of whether it is stated in words, many parents intentionally withhold their blessing until their children prove themselves worthy or start conducting themselves in an acceptable manner. It's as if we

THE BLESSING GIVEN TO A CHILD AT THE TRANSITION POINT INTO ADULTHOOD WAS LIKE A DOORWAY A CHILD WOULD PASS THROUGH.

are saying, "When you dress, talk, and conduct yourself in a manner that pleases me, I will bless you."

## What Are We Really Communicating?

When we withhold the blessing (pending our personal approval), we teach our children that they can manipulate us and God. The concept is simple. From a very young age we teach our children what it takes to make us happy—their actions, their attitudes, their conduct. In doing so, we also teach them what makes us unhappy. By withholding the blessing, we think we are controlling them, when in reality we are teaching them that they can control us and our feelings.

> BY WITHHOLDING THE BLESSING, WE THINK WE ARE CONTROLLING THEM, WHEN IN REALITY WE ARE TEACHING THEM THAT THEY CAN CONTROL US AND OUR FEELINGS.

I have come to believe that part of what is termed "teenage rebellion" isn't rebellion at all. It is our children crying out for us to stop controlling them and instead love them for who they are. It boils down to this: Even as Christians we have learned to bless good behavior and withhold blessing for bad behavior. God blesses his children for who they are—not for what they do. It is certainly true that God rewards obedience, but he also blesses us simply because we are his children. You see, God's blessings focus on a future and a destiny, while we have allowed our blessings as parents to focus on good behavior. One looks forward, while the other looks back.

> THE BLESSING HAS BECOME A REWARD FOR GOOD BEHAVIOR, FOR BEHAVIOR THAT'S PLEASING OR ACCEPTABLE TO US.

To help our children keep their faith, we must learn to bless their future and their destiny; we must help them focus on where they're going, not where they've been; we must use the blessing to unlock the shackles of their past instead of tightening them until our kids change in a manner that pleases us.

Do you know the power of your words as a parent? Specifically, do you know the power of your words as a blessing connecting your child to his or her future and destiny? Understanding God's blessing can transform us. It's the difference between a past and a future, between freedom and imprisonment, and between hope and condemnation.

### "Will Anybody Pray for Me?"

Several years ago at Ft. Leonard Wood, Missouri, we conducted a rite of passage. This was a unique experience because it included people from various faith groups and chaplains from at least six different denominations. One by one the young men and women were called into the sanctuary, where they received a blessing from their parents or spiritual parents and then a blessing from the chaplains representing all the chapels of Ft. Leonard Wood. The ceremony had just drawn to a close, and there was still an excitement in the air, when I witnessed something I had never seen before.

As one of the chaplains walked up the aisle, a young man stepped out in front of him, communicating by his body language, "You're not getting past me until we take care of this." I later found out the young man was a high school senior and a star football player. The words he spoke, however, came from a young man who—in witnessing a ceremony for others—realized his own need. Tears formed in his eyes as he said to the chaplain, "You don't know me—I'm not from here. I'm not military and my family isn't military. I'm just here with my girlfriend. But I understand everything that took place tonight. Will anybody pray for me?" With that he dropped to his knees, directly in front of the chaplain. He wasn't moving until he received what was given to the other young men and women. It was as if he were saying, "I have a future and a destiny too. Will you help connect me to it?"

When we bless our children we say to them, in essence, "You have an incredible future and a destiny. As your parent I want to bless you and connect you with the power you need in order to walk in the fullness of who God created you to be."

## FOR PERSONAL REFLECTION OR GROUP DISCUSSION

After reading this chapter and considering the study questions, we encourage you to prepare a written "blessing" for your children.

1. Read Genesis 27:1–29 and review the five critical elements of a "family blessing" as defined by Smalley and Trent. What is the most important issue that stands out to you?

2. What do you pray that God will do as you bless your child?

3. How would you state your child's high value to you and God?

4. Can you picture a special future for your son or daughter? Describe it.

5. How can you actively support and seek to fulfill the blessing of your child?

6. How does the blessing shape your child's future and destiny?

7. Pray that God will allow you to see your son or daughter with his eyes in order to know how to prepare the blessing for your child—and his.

# PART 4

## "EVEN GENERATIONS YET TO BE BORN ..."

## CHAPTER 18

# LEGACY OR JUST ANOTHER LEGEND?

On a glorious spring day in St. Louis, I sat in Busch Memorial Stadium for the opening day of the 1998 Major League Baseball season. For baseball fans, the atmosphere couldn't have been better. Much of the preseason talk had centered on Mark McGwire and whether he would hit enough home runs that year to set a new Major League record. Late in the game, with the bases loaded, McGwire stepped to the plate. With all eyes on him, the slugger delivered what everyone had come to see—the first of the seventy record-setting home runs he would hit that season. The stadium erupted with cheers that continued even after he rounded the bases and returned to the dugout.

A few moments later, as we finally settled back into our seats, the gentleman sitting next to me turned and asked me a question. Perhaps he felt compelled based on the message I had spoken earlier that day at the mayor's prayer breakfast in Granite City, Illinois. He said, "Chuck, what do you think the legacy of Mark McGwire will be?"

I paused for a moment, pondering his question, and then replied, "I don't think that's really your question. What you are really asking is what I think the final *legend* of Mark McGwire will be." Then I reiterated what I had said earlier in the day: "We live in a world that talks all the time about legacies but in reality focuses on legends. Legends are made by the things people do and the stories that are told about them. A legacy, however, is established by who we are—the fiber and fabric that's passed on to future generations."

Although the man had asked what I thought McGwire's legacy would be, what he was actually interested in was how many home runs the slugger would hit that year and how many records he would break before his baseball career was over. We are taught by our society to think of "leaving a legacy" in terms of accomplishments. What people do and accumulate comprises their legend, however, which will normally only have value until it is surpassed by something or someone else.

I went on to say, "I'm not sure about Mark McGwire's legacy because that will be determined by the quality of man he is—the fiber and fabric of which he is made. Not knowing McGwire personally, I can't make that assessment. While it's easy to speculate about the legend—the individual records and accomplishments—it's far more difficult to determine the legacy."

Since this conversation several years ago, the question of McGwire's legacy—along with that of many other baseball celebrities, past and present—has come under intense public scrutiny. As I write this, in the days following congressional hearings pertaining to steroid use in baseball, I wonder what the man I sat next to on the opening day of the 1998 season is thinking now about McGwire's legacy compared to his legend.

## Psalm 78:5-7: My "Legacy Verses"

Within moments after her birth in a Denver hospital on March 3, 1998, I held in my arms my first grandchild. To say that there was something supernatural about that moment would understate the reality. It's been said that a child of your child is twice your child, and now I understand why. In the weeks preceding and the days following the birth of Eliana Blair Cassel, God gave me incredible clarity about what's important to pass on through the generations. I was particularly struck by Psalm 78:5-7:

> He decreed statutes for Jacob and established the law in Israel, which he commanded our forefathers to teach their children, so the next generation would know them, even the children yet to be born, and they in turn would tell their children. Then they would

put their trust in God and would not forget his deeds but would keep his commands.

As I read those verses, it was as if neon lights began blinking and flashing, and bells and whistles went off. Everything in my being seemed to cry out, "This is what it means to leave a godly legacy!" I declared Psalm 78:5–7 to be my "legacy verses" that moment and determined I would teach about them whenever I had the opportunity.

Notice the number of generations mentioned here in just three verses. The process begins with the law given to Israel (Jacob) through Moses (generation one); Israel would teach their children (generation two), and those children would then teach the next generation—"the children yet to be born" (generation three), who would in turn teach their children (generation four).

Notice also that God spoke three things to be taught through the generations—to trust, remember, and obey the living God. I realized that as much as dads want to control the destiny of their children (I have jokingly said on many occasions that my grandchildren will live in Denver, and I don't care where their parents live), I began to understand in that final verse exactly what comprises the legacy of Almighty God in our lives, our children's lives, and our children's children's lives.

Seventeen months after the birth of Eliana, Hannah Marie Cassel was born. Within minutes of her birth, I held her in my arms, as I had her older sister. And as we had done with Eliana, the entire family gathered close as we dedicated her life to the God who had created her. My prayer for her on August 12, 1999, was that we (her family) would help her grow into a woman who would trust, remember, and obey the living God.

## Losing Control

If you have ever thought that you had control over the lives of your children, it doesn't take very much to show you that you don't. Within a couple years after Hannah's birth, I would have a son and daughter-in-law living in Kansas and a son in the army in Washington, D.C.

Even though our family is close and we talk regularly and continue to pray with and for each other, it doesn't take a genius to figure out that I had very little control in their lives.

When your children move out, you may heave a great sigh of relief. On the other hand, you might feel a bit fearful. I realize my children remembered God many times because Billie and I reminded them to, trusted God because we did, and obeyed God because we had chosen to do so as a family. But now they were on their own. No longer would it be a case of them remembering, trusting, and obeying God because their father and mother did—now it was a choice they made for themselves.

In the two years since all of our children left home, I've thought countless times about the energy I spent helping them understand what to do, and I've wondered about how much more I could have done to help them understand who they are. Our children are great—and by all standards they're doing terrifically well. That doesn't mean I still haven't wondered what I could have done better. Now, with grandchildren, it is as if God has given me a "do over" in some of the areas I feel I should have done better as a father.

## Back to the Starting Line—Rites of Passage

Perhaps you're wondering why rites of passage are so important. It's because the rite of passage into adulthood is a defining moment that marks the line between childhood faith and adult faith. Without it, that line becomes blurred. Too often, young people have no connection to an adult faith.

Several years ago I had a conversation with a man who was the father of a teenage son. He felt as though he had failed his children. He told me that a year earlier his son had been very active in church, youth group, and Sunday school. It was now a struggle just to get him to church, and the man wasn't even sure his son believed in God at all. He said it was as if the boy were two different sons, raised in two different homes. I explained that his son was becoming a man—no longer a child in the family but a young man in the family. In becoming a young man, he was leaving his childhood faith and searching for his adult faith.

The faith of a child is his or her parents' faith, but the faith of an adult is his or her own. I tried to help this father understand that his son was leaving behind his childish ways. (See 1 Cor. 13:11.) He was leaving behind and struggling with his childhood faith that he had held because it was his parents' and he had wanted to make them happy. He was searching for the faith he could live with as an adult. Many of our children make this transition seamlessly, while others seem to wrestle with it for an eternity. I suggested to this dad that he had an incredible opportunity to help his son grow and find his own faith.

THE RITE OF PASSAGE INTO ADULTHOOD IS A DEFINING MOMENT THAT MARKS THE LINE BETWEEN CHILDHOOD FAITH AND ADULT FAITH.

## Leaving a Legacy

*Webster's Dictionary* defines a legacy as "something of value that is passed on to another generation."[1] What is there of greater value to pass to each generation than their own faith in God? We can begin to recognize the true objective. The journey's end now cries out to us. The objective is to help our sons and daughters become godly men and women. For them to have a faith in the living God as adults and not believe simply because their parents believe, we have to ask the question, how can they have an adult faith if they have never become adults? Actually the question is, how can they grow with an adult faith in homes and churches that have never recognized them as adults? The picture comes into sharper focus when we realize the only place most of our children are recognized as adults is in the secular world—a world that recognizes them as adults but tells them there is no place or need for their faith. Conversely, in many of our homes and churches we want them to have an adult faith, but we refuse to recognize them as adults.

Legend or legacy—you make the call. Choosing a legend means you are asking your children to live a life that makes you proud.

Choosing a legacy means you want to help your children come into their own faith as godly young men and women who no longer rely on their parents' faith.

A man's legend reflects what he has accomplished and collected. God's legacy centers on preparing our children to teach their children to trust, remember, and obey the living God.

## FOR PERSONAL REFLECTION OR GROUP DISCUSSION

1. After reading this chapter, would you say that you have been focused on your *legend* or your *legacy?*

2. Reread Psalm 78:5–7. How does your definition of legacy compare to God's desire as stated in these verses?

3. If you are considering your true legacy, how have your thoughts changed?

4. What steps should you take to begin creating your own godly legacy?

5. Can you think of any way that would help your children have an adult faith of their own if you have never recognized them as adults? How, then, can rites of passage into adulthood for your children impact your legacy?

## CHAPTER 19

# BRING YOUR RUNNERS TO THE STARTING LINE

We've all seen or participated in many different types of racing events. Let's take a moment to think about four specific types of footraces.

The first category is track events. The course is a 400-meter oval track. Many years ago, I ran the quarter-mile. The surface of the running area is smooth and without obstacles. The lanes are clearly marked. The intervals for the distance run and still to be run are easy to determine.

The second type is a cross-country race. Although these races aren't run on a level track, the running area is well-groomed and usually not very complicated. And although you don't always know exactly how far you've run and how far you have yet to go, in most cases at least some interval distances are marked. I'm sure most runners find a cross-country race to be mentally more difficult to run than a track race.

The third type of race is a marathon, so called because of a legendary messenger who ran from the ancient village of Marathon in Greece to Athens in 490 BC to announce a victory over the Persians. The modern marathon distance—26 miles and 385 yards—was set for the 1908 London Olympics so the course could start at Windsor Castle and end in front of the royal box. Not until 1921, however, was that distance adopted as the "official" marathon distance by the International Association of Athletics Federations. Obviously, you have to be well prepared both physically and mentally to run a marathon. But at least the course, typically paved streets, is clearly marked, and the route includes regular signs designating distance intervals—keeping the runners informed of how far they've run and how far they have yet to go.

The fourth type of race is an assortment of demanding events known as ultramarathons, lovingly referred to by some as "ultras." These events come in quite a wide variety with only one thing in common: The distance is longer (usually significantly longer) than a marathon. One particular kind of ultramarathon is a whole different type of animal. The distance of the race often exceeds one hundred miles and is such that participants can't possibly run the entire race during daylight. The route is not marked. There might be, in fact, several options for covering the distance. There are various obstacles, such as rocks, ruts, and creeks—things runners must go over, under, or around. It is grueling and, needless to say, those who compete get pretty dirty.

## The Parenting Race

Most of us parents would like childrearing to be similar to a track race, where we can run on an oval track in perfectly marked lanes, anticipating the next lap, and seeing exactly how far we've come and how far we have yet to go. It's also appealing to us to have race officials watching closely so other runners can't intentionally knock us off the track, trip us, or impede us. This seems ideal for the launching of children into adulthood—smooth running and free of obstacles.

Many of us are okay with a parenting experience that's similar to the cross-country race—and even the marathon. We know the race will be tough, but at least we have a good idea of what we're getting into. Our footing is secure, and the course is well marked. Though portions of the course are uphill, we know we'll be able to glide a bit on the backside. We don't need to worry much about other runners cutting us off or impeding our path. While we would prefer the simple oval track, we can accept the cross-country or marathon course because we still have a fair understanding of how far we've come and how far we have yet to go. The entire distance will be covered in daylight hours and certainly should not be life threatening.

A far more realistic picture of parenting, however, is the last type of race—the grueling ultramarathon whose distance cannot be covered in daylight hours and is filled with many obstacles. Even the most well-prepared runner in this race can't anticipate some of the obstacles he or she will face. At times in this kind of ultramarathon you may even be clueless as to how far you've traveled and how far you have yet to go. There is nothing that even compares to it.

If you've ever watched a marathon, you know there are tables with water and nourishment set up throughout the course. You often see the runners grabbing a beverage cup as they continue running. It takes guts to finish a marathon, but it's pretty tough to get lost! The ultramarathon is the only type of race in which runners might lose their way.

## Preparing Our Children for the "Race"

As parents, the challenge is not just about being able to run the extreme ultramarathon ourselves; it's also about preparing our children to run that race as well. As I stated in chapter 11, there are two constants in any race: Regardless of the type of race, the type of course, or the distance, there is always an established starting line and an established finish line.

EVEN THE MOST WELL-PREPARED RUNNER IN THIS RACE CAN'T ANTICIPATE SOME OF THE OBSTACLES HE OR SHE WILL FACE.

As a parent, the rite of passage into adulthood is like taking your son or daughter to the starting line for an extreme ultramarathon race. The moment just before your child approaches the starting line is different from anything else you've done before or will ever do again. As your daughter stands there waiting to be called to the starting line, you're checking to make sure her shoes are tied properly and double knotted. You talk her through her strategy and remind her that it isn't the same as running around the block a couple of times.

As she gets ready to begin this race, you get to pin her number on her—indicating she is an official contestant. Mom and Dad, brothers and sisters, and other family members can gather around to give words of encouragement and pray a blessing on her. It's a time when your pastor stops by for a moment to speak words of encouragement and pray a blessing. He lets her know how proud he is of her and how good it is for their church to have another runner in this race.

### Prerace Instructions

Now here comes the really good part. This is where we, as parents, get to look into our son's or daughter's eyes and say, "We have done everything we can do to prepare you for this time. We have tried to tell you in advance where the obstacles will be and how you can overcome them. We have tried to help you understand the markings on the trail that will indicate you're going in the right direction. We have tried to explain to you how to identify the distance markers and how to know when you're going from one portion of the race to another—over different terrain and challenges."

As you hold your son or daughter, you say, "This doesn't mean I'm leaving you or that you'll have to run the race on your own. It means that, unlike your childhood days when virtually everything you did could be observed by your parents, it might appear to you that you're all alone. But that isn't the case. There will be checkpoints in the race where we'll be waiting for you. You might look up and see your older brother or sister standing on the sidelines, cheering you on. There will be times when none of your immediate family can be there, but if you look around you may see someone from the body of Christ encouraging you or trying to help you overcome obstacles that we didn't anticipate. It may be one of the men or women of our church, it may be one of your peers, or it may be the mother or father of a friend."

Continuing on, you say, "As you run this race of life, you'll find that some areas are easy and some are very difficult. But as your parents and your church family, we're going to spread ourselves out over this course. We are going to meet you at every place we can to encourage and lift you. Here is the key issue for this race—the victory doesn't go to the one who finishes first, but to all who complete the course. The fact that you are in this race now as an adult doesn't mean you can't ask for help. In fact, you can help other runners, too."

The start time is drawing near now. You see other runners moving to the starting line. You see other families assembled—parents, grandparents, aunts, uncles, brothers, and sisters—blessing their children. The final thing you want your son or daughter to know is this: "We believe in you. We trust you will run this race in your own style, using your God-given gifts. We believe you'll run this race to completion. Run with courage, help others along the way as God enables you, and finish strong."

"HERE IS THE KEY ISSUE FOR THIS RACE— THE VICTORY DOESN'T GO TO THE ONE WHO FINISHES FIRST, BUT TO ALL WHO COMPLETE THE COURSE."

## FOR PERSONAL REFLECTION OR GROUP DISCUSSION

1. Does parenting seem more like a track event, cross-country race, marathon, or ultramarathon to you?

2. How have you begun to prepare your children for the race of life after they no longer live in your home?

3. What do you consider to be the critical prerace instructions for your son or daughter?

4. In a highly competitive world, how do you assure your kids that the victory goes to all who compete and finish—not just to the one who finishes first?

## chapter 20

# DEVELOPING THE COMMUNITY OF COACHES AND ENCOURAGERS

Most dads reading this probably think they're tougher than Superman's kneecap and Chinese arithmetic. I like to portray the same image. But I can't watch a scene from the Special Olympics without tearing up. There's something about the atmosphere of the entire event that grabs your heart and won't let it go.

### What Makes the Special Olympics so Special?

Three factors work together for the express purpose of making each participant in the Special Olympics successful: the coaches, the encouragers, and, last but not least, the community surrounding the event.

Coaches are recruited to help all participants increase their skills in the particular events in which they are participating. Other people are recruited just for the specific purpose of being encouragers. It's like every contestant has his or her own pit crew. Finally, the community as a whole is nothing short of amazing—as each and every participant is cheered on wildly. I love the term "Special Olympics" because every one of the participants is truly special.

The parents of Special Olympians will guide their children to coaches and will help them recruit encouragers—often from their own pool of friends. When a person agrees to become an encourager, he is no longer there as a friend to the parent; he is there because of the

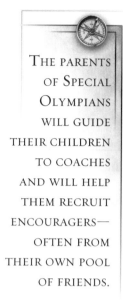

**THE PARENTS OF SPECIAL OLYMPIANS WILL GUIDE THEIR CHILDREN TO COACHES AND WILL HELP THEM RECRUIT ENCOURAGERS— OFTEN FROM THEIR OWN POOL OF FRIENDS.**

relationship he has with the participant. Encouragers come in all shapes and sizes, transcending gender and generational lines. What's critical is that they share the values of the contestant, the contestant's family, and the entire Special Olympics community.

Once a Special Olympian has coaches and encouragers and has become part of the community, the situation goes beyond sports—it becomes a lifestyle. Have you ever considered that maybe, just maybe, this is what the church family is supposed to be like, and that we, as parents, all have special children— each and every one?

One of the greatest things we can do for our children is not just agree with God about their adulthood, but develop around them the coaches, encouragers, and community that will help them grow, mature, and keep their faith. When it comes to coaches and encouragers, it is essential that we release our friends to become their friends.

## A Special Coach

In 1994 I joined the staff of Promise Keepers and had the privilege of meeting Bill McCartney, who was then still the head football coach at the University of Colorado. During my first few years on staff, Bill continued coaching and, as his schedule would permit, spoke at various Promise Keepers events. I met him on several occasions, but it wasn't until after he became the president of Promise Keepers and worked from the national offices that I actually got to know him. On several occasions when I saw Bill, I had both my sons with me. And each time I gave them the opportunity to say hello to the man who had become my friend. What I didn't realize was that, over time, they came to consider him their own friend. To this day, if they're in the same location, they'll seek him out and speak with him.

One Saturday morning in the spring of 1996 I took Chad and Courtney to the Promise Keepers office with me. We were sitting in my office area when Bill walked by and said hello to all three of us. We talked for a few minutes, and then he continued on to his office.

After a few minutes my younger son, Courtney, who was in sixth grade at the time, told me he was going to Coach's office to talk to him about something. I was somewhat concerned because I knew Bill wasn't coming to the office on a Saturday morning just to sit there and wait to see who stopped by to visit with him. Since I wanted to be respectful of his time, I cautioned Courtney not to stay too long. He looked back and gave me a smile, as if to say, "I'm going to see *my* friend—not yours."

As time passed I became increasingly concerned, until Courtney finally came around the corner. He immediately asked me to stop by Bill's office on Monday because Bill's administrative assistant would have a package for him. Unaware of what had just transpired, I asked Courtney what I was going to be picking up for him. He looked at me and matter-of-factly said, "Coach is loaning me the jacket and hat he wore for the last college game he coached."

I must have had a puzzled look on my face because Courtney (out of kindness) went on to explain that he was giving a book report at school on Coach's autobiography, *From Ashes to Glory*. The teacher was requiring the students to dress the part of the person they had chosen as the subject of their book report. Bill McCartney was a major figure in Colorado at the time. He probably could have run for governor and been elected by a landslide. Imagine a sixth grader standing before his class and giving a report about the football coach who had led the Colorado Buffaloes to a national championship! Now imagine that sixth grader wearing the jacket and hat the coach had worn in his last game. I'm not sure Courtney even needed to give the book report! To say Bill McCartney was an encourager to my sons, and on this occasion specifically to my younger son, would be similar to announcing that the sun is hot.

## Making My Friends Their Friends

It occurred to me some time ago that one thing I could do to help my children and their spouses, as well as their children, grow to be men of honor and women of virtue was to release my friends to also be their friends. I believe all parents need to do this. By doing so, we show our children how to pick their own coaches and encouragers.

The coaches, encouragers, and community we need to develop around our children are normally within a handshake of our own lives and can cross gender and generational lines. As we recognize what God has done in making our children adults, we must commit to helping them learn about adult relationships. Many of us have heard it said, "Show me your friends, and I will show you your future."

## Holy Huddles

Several months ago, the night before a rite of passage in Lee's Summit, Missouri, I witnessed one of those extraordinary moments only God could orchestrate. We'd gathered that evening for a time of prayer. The young men and women who would participate in the rite of passage the following evening were invited to come and kneel at the front of the church if they felt there was any area of their lives in which they needed God to restore purity.

With no emotional plea or coercion, young men and women filled the front of the church. As the lights were dimmed and soft music played, seven senior boys from the local high school came together and placed their arms around each other's shoulders. It looked as if God was pulling together a holy huddle and creating a team. When the evening drew to a close, everyone else was finished except for the seven young men still locked in their holy huddle. As they continued to pray for one another, God stirred the hearts of some men in the church who, without saying a word, created a second holy huddle around the seven young men. Through prayer, God moved to intertwine the lives of all the men involved.

When the time of prayer was finished, the young men looked up to see the faces and feel the arms of the men who had gathered around them. These older men were no longer their fathers' friends or just some men from the church, but in a miraculous moment God had made all of these men friends—regardless of age—and many of them continue to walk in close relationships today.

## Filling the Gap after Columbine

I was in Nashville when the Columbine shootings took place and couldn't get home for a couple of days. Knowing I was out of town, my good friend and Christian brother Gary Sallquist immediately instructed his administrative assistant to cancel all his appointments. He then called my wife from his home in Colorado Springs to ask if our guest room was available. He wanted to be there in my absence to be available to a couple of his friends—my sons, Chad and Courtney.

I wasn't able to be physically present with my sons, but fortunately one of their friends was there—an older man who loved them and didn't consider them as much my sons as his friends. In the crucial hours and days that followed, Gary walked in the park near the high school with Chad and Courtney, who were hurting and confused. They had many friends at Columbine, including several of the victims. As only another man could do, Gary provided my sons a safe environment in which to be men—an opportunity to cry and to question.

Gary and I have been friends for almost forty years. Gary and my sons have been friends for far less time, but it certainly doesn't diminish the strength of their friendship.

One of the most incredible results I've witnessed in close to sixty rites of passage in local churches has been the nearly instantaneous development of community around the young men and women. One of our primary responsibilities as parents is to help develop that community around our children. Where it doesn't exist, we need to initiate the concept of community based on common values and shared trusts. And we must teach our children how to nurture and develop that community for themselves in the future.

> AS ONLY ANOTHER MAN COULD DO, GARY PROVIDED MY SONS A SAFE ENVIRONMENT IN WHICH TO BE MEN—AN OPPORTUNITY TO CRY AND TO QUESTION.

# FOR PERSONAL REFLECTION OR GROUP DISCUSSION

1. In your mind, what makes the Special Olympics so special?

2. What can you do to develop the coaches, encouragers, and community that will help your children grow, mature, and keep their own faith?

3. Name three of your own friends with whom you could encourage your son or daughter to develop a friendship.

4. What should you be doing now to ensure that in a time of tragedy your friends would fill the gap for your kids if you were not there?

## CHAPTER 21

# RUN THE RACE TO THE FINISH LINE

In 1926, twenty-year-old Gertrude "Trudy" Ederle completed the twenty-one-mile swim across the English Channel. Trudy was a remarkable person who inspired thousands with her story of determination, courage, and tenacity.

Swimming the English Channel is no ordinary feat today and was even more difficult in 1926. The channel is a harsh place at best. The bitterly cold water has incredibly strong currents and waves frequently exceeding twenty feet high. It is often subject to high winds and fog. In addition, the water teems with jellyfish of the Portuguese man-of-war type, and on occasion sharks are seen. It is also a primary shipping lane, so swimmers must always be alert for freighters.

In 1926, only five persons—all of them men—had accomplished the feat. It was unthinkable for a woman to attempt the swim and inconceivable that a woman could actually complete it.

To make matters worse, Trudy Ederle had challenged the channel a year earlier and had been pulled from the water by her coach when a wave engulfed her and she stopped swimming momentarily. She would later state that at the time she was pulled from the water she had no idea how close she was to reaching the shore. Had Trudy known she only had six miles to go, she might have been able to keep going and complete the swim on her first attempt.

Preparing for the second attempt was far more difficult than for the first. Mentally, the second time was much tougher because she had already been beaten once. She would have to be able to complete the swim mentally before she could do it physically. She may have been shaken, but she wasn't defeated.

There would be another price to pay as well. The Women's Swimming Association had funded her first attempt but was unable to sponsor her second attempt. The *Chicago Tribune* offered to finance the second attempt, but if she accepted the money she would lose her amateur status for any further competition. Ederle had already won three medals at the 1924 Olympics and had set twenty-nine U.S. and world records by the time she was nineteen. Giving up her amateur status was not an easy decision. She decided to accept the offer, however, because her goal to swim the English Channel was more important than winning more medals.

Adding to the doubt concerning Ederle's second attempt was the stroke she decided to use. All five men who had successfully crossed the channel had used the breaststroke. She decided to use a new stroke called the crawl, which she had learned swimming in a New Jersey river as a child.

None of these issues would matter when Trudy Ederle climbed out of the water on August 6, 1926, and became the first woman to successfully swim the English Channel. Her time of fourteen hours and thirty-one minutes broke the record of the fastest male swimmer by nearly two hours! Her time would stand as the female record for nearly thirty-five years.

Preparing for the second attempt, Trudy Ederle knew she could not do everything the same way she had the first time and expect a different result. She concentrated on four areas that had to change:

1. *The Plan.* Her first attempt was based on the plans of others. Her second attempt was *her* plan based on her unique abilities.

2. *The Coach.* Trudy's first coach had attempted the swim himself twenty times without success. Her coach for the second attempt was Thomas Burgess, one of the five men who had successfully swum the channel.

3. *The Encouragers*. Ederle knew she would need encouragers if she was to overcome the memory of her failed first attempt. Near her was a small tugboat containing her coach, her father, her sister, and several good friends—all cheering her on. Farther back was a boat containing the press.

4. *The Decision*. On her first attempt, Trudy's coach thought she had swallowed too much salt water and felt she could not continue. The moment he touched her to pull her out of the water, she was disqualified and the swim was over. On the second attempt, Ederle and her new coach had an understanding that no one could touch her or pull her out unless she agreed. Twelve hours into the swim, when the ocean was churning violently, her coach told her she had to stop. Trudy merely replied, "What for?"

Let's look at how Trudy Ederle's attempts to swim the English Channel can speak to us, as parents, about raising our kids to "keep the faith."

## The Plan

Trudy used the same plan in her first attempt that was used by all the other swimmers who had attempted to swim the channel. The plan Trudy chose for her second attempt was suited just for her. Parents too often look for cookie-cutter plans for raising godly, successful kids. Granted, there are specific, uniform goals that need to be accomplished along the life journey of any child and adult, but there are different ways to get there.

Christian parents nearly always agree that God created their children with their own gifting and purpose. We each want the same thing for our children—that they be successful in life—but too often we gauge success by the world's standards. I remember talking to a young man who was assisting me with my computers. I casually asked him where he graduated from high school—normally a standard question to help establish a common frame of reference. He looked at me and responded that he *didn't* graduate from high school. He must have seen the shock on my face, because I knew he had graduated from college.

Probably as a courtesy to save me from any more verbal fumbling, he explained that high school was boring for him. He loved computers, but he hated high school. When he was sixteen he asked his parents if he could drop out of high school. Before they could say no and explain why that wouldn't be a good idea, he shared with them that he had already picked a local college that would accept him if he completed his General Education Diploma (GED). He and his parents agreed that if he passed his GED exam he could quit high school and go to college.

Within a few weeks he passed the exam and enrolled in a local college. At the age of eighteen, while his classmates were graduating from high school, he was graduating from a two-year college in a field in which he excelled. And today he is doing what he truly loves.

I'm not suggesting that we encourage or even allow our children to drop out of high school at age sixteen. But I am suggesting that we should have a plan that uniquely fits each of them and the special gifts God has given them.

The example I just shared comes from the field of education. We have a similar situation in most of our churches. The only Christian education classes available for many of our teens are the high school or junior high Sunday school classes, when in fact many of our teens, if given the opportunity, would rather be part of a subject-specific class that's normally reserved for the so-called adults of the church.

Throughout this book I have endeavored to identify the need for intergenerational relationships. I don't think it's too great a stretch for parents to be able to see the benefit of their teenage sons and daughters sitting in their church's adult education classes.

The bottom line is this: The plan to raise our kids to keep the faith really must be a plan to help them keep *their* faith rather than our faith.

## The Coach

Trudy Ederle's first coach had attempted to swim the English Channel on twenty different occasions but had never completed the swim successfully. He pulled Trudy out of the water when he believed she was at the point where *he* could not have continued the swim.

On her second attempt, she knew she had to have a coach who knew what it was like to step out of the channel on the other side. Even though her second coach had attempted the swim thirteen times before he finally succeeded, his failures were never remembered. It was the success that was in the record books, making him, at the time, one of only five men to complete the swim.

I don't think I can emphasize enough how critical it is that we help our kids get the right coaches. They need coaches who will not give up on them. We aren't released from the responsibility of good parenting, but we do our children a terrible injustice if we don't work hard to help them find life coaches as well.

When it comes to athletics, we have no trouble seeing the value of an experienced coach. We want even better coaches as our children become older and more proficient at a given sport. Yet when it comes to life, we often don't see the value of the coaches who can bring a different experience level and relationship into the lives of our children. I am constantly looking for opportunities to expand my children's coaching teams. That may sound strange in light of the fact that two of my children are married and the other one is in the U.S. Army—and therefore all three are living out of our home.

My wife and I have a plan for raising our children in their faith that goes far beyond the day they moved out of our home. It will continue until God calls us "home" to heaven. As a result of this concept, there are people around our sons and daughter who began as friends of Billie and me but through the years developed their own relationship with our children. I could fill several pages in this book with the names of men and women our sons and daughter have known who began as their parents' friends and became their life coaches.

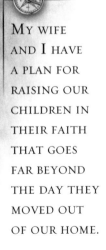

I DON'T THINK I CAN EMPHASIZE ENOUGH HOW CRITICAL IT IS THAT WE HELP OUR KIDS GET THE RIGHT COACHES.

MY WIFE AND I HAVE A PLAN FOR RAISING OUR CHILDREN IN THEIR FAITH THAT GOES FAR BEYOND THE DAY THEY MOVED OUT OF OUR HOME.

## The Encouragers

The third area in which Trudy made a major change was realizing her encouragers must be close enough to encourage. On the first attempt, it was all about the press—they were the closest ones to her, except for her coach who had never completed the swim himself. The problem was that many members of the press didn't believe she could complete the swim and were actually there to see her fail.

That changed when the closest boat accompanying her on the second swim contained her coach who had finished the swim, her father, her sister, and other encouragers. She even had them bring a phonograph to play her favorite songs. At times they all sang along. What a difference it makes when the closest "boat" to us is filled with people who believe in us and believe that we can finish the race—leaving the naysayers to follow along at a safe distance!

WHAT A DIFFERENCE IT MAKES WHEN THE CLOSEST "BOAT" TO US IS FILLED WITH PEOPLE WHO BELIEVE IN US AND BELIEVE THAT WE CAN FINISH THE RACE.

We begin the race of life with God the Father, who says, "Never will I leave you; never will I forsake you" (Heb. 13:5), and "There is a friend who sticks closer than a brother" (Prov. 18:24), and Jesus who said, "I am with you always" (Matt. 28:20).

As I mentioned in the last chapter, in the early stages we need to help our children pick their encouragers and develop those relationships. In other words, we fill the stands with cheerleaders for our children. My daughter and son-in-law are in their thirties; my two sons and daughter-in-law are in their twenties. To this day I still take advantage of every opportunity I have to fill their stands with cheerleaders. There are plenty of people in the world who will tell my children that they cannot succeed. I want to line the streets of their lives with men and women who will shout from the rooftops that they *can* succeed.

One of the greatest benefits we have seen from nearly sixty rites of passage across the country is how many of the churches have become the cheering squad for their young men and women. What better place for that to happen?

Over and over I have shared examples of the church being the community and family of God. It has become a safe place for our sons and daughters primarily because it has become a source of encouragement.

## The Decision

The decision to stop Trudy's initial attempt to swim the English Channel was made by her coach. She didn't consciously give him the authority to make that decision before the swim; but because she hadn't prepared for it, the decision inadvertently fell into his hands. Trudy didn't leave that decision to chance on her second attempt. She decided before the swim that she, and she alone, would decide if she was to be pulled from the water short of achieving her objective.

FRANKLY, TOO MANY PARENTS GIVE UP ON THEIR CHILDREN BASED ON ILL-CONCEIVED ADVICE THAT THERE IS NOTHING ELSE THEY CAN DO.

Frankly, too many parents give up on their children based on ill-conceived advice that there is nothing else they can do. Granted, at times all you have is prayer, but often all you *need* is prayer. I take advice all the time concerning medical, financial, or ministry issues. I take advice as to what is best for my children and what I can do to improve my marriage. But mind you, it is only advice. The decision to keep going is mine.

We either believe in God or we deny God—there is no in-between. All too often we try to walk in the shadows between the two possibilities. Since God is our Creator and our Father, I believe he will direct our paths. He desires what is best for his children whom he has entrusted to our care. To the unspiritual eye, his direction will sometimes seem like abandonment, because he will tell us to take *our* hands off our children so he can place *his* hands on them. Sometimes the most difficult option is to trust God and do nothing else. Ultimately the decision rests in our hands. Never quit!

If we are serious about the need for our children to keep their faith, then we must do everything necessary to give them that opportunity. If we're content with raising "good kids," then we'll try our best to have them keep *our* faith. But if we truly want to see them walk in the fullness of who they are and who God created them to be, we will recognize their adulthood, release them from our faith, and help them find *their* faith.

> Not that I have already obtained all this, or have already been made perfect, but I press on to take hold of that for which Christ Jesus took hold of me. Brothers, I do not consider myself yet to have taken hold of it. But one thing I do: Forgetting what is behind and straining toward what is ahead, I press on toward the goal to win the prize for which God has called me heavenward in Christ Jesus. (Phil. 3:12–14)

## FOR PERSONAL REFLECTION OR GROUP DISCUSSION

1. How would you describe your plan for helping your son or daughter become spiritually mature? Does it include helping them to avoid the mistakes that you made?

2. In what areas of life do your children already need specialized coaches? Are you helping them find those coaches?

3. How does your church function as the encouragers your kids need? How can you help your church recognize and respond to this need?

4. This chapter stated that we need to take *our* hands off our children so that God can place *his* hands on them. Why is this one of the most difficult things for even the best parents to do?

5. Take a moment, in prayer, to recommit your children to God's care and purpose.

## chapter 22

# EXPECT THE BEST

In 1961 John Gardner wrote a book titled *Excellence*. I have kept my tattered copy—with the pages falling out and held together with a rubber band—near my desk for many, many years.

Mr. Gardner related a story that, in my estimation, provides a key to helping parents teach their children to keep the faith.

> We are beginning to understand that the various kinds of talents that flower in any society are the kinds that are valued in the society. On a recent visit to Holland, my wife asked a Dutchwoman why children and adults in that country showed such an extraordinary high incidence of language skills. "We expect it of children," the woman said simply. "We think it important."[1]

As parents, churches, and a society, we seem to have lost track of how much our children respond to what we value. Our children can see the difference between what we say is important and what we genuinely value. In all too many cases, what we say is important only applies to them as we try to mold and shape their lives—whereas the things that are truly important to us can be validated by looking at our checkbooks, our calendars, and our hearts.

## A Mother's Passing

I was invited to speak at a pastor's luncheon in Alexandria, Louisiana, about three years ago. As we introduced ourselves to one another before the program began, I had the privilege of meeting a pastor from the area. His name is not widely known; his church numbers fewer than seventy people. Yet the power of his presence was as great as that of any man I have ever met. This pastor told me he had just buried his mother the day before. There was a joy in his voice that transcended the pain he felt at his loss.

I asked him to tell me about the funeral. (You can determine a lot about a family by how they celebrate the births and deaths of their loved ones.) Within moments I was captivated by the story the pastor related. Beginning two nights earlier at the wake, in addition to the gathering of family and friends, fourteen pastors came to be with the family and celebrate the home-going of his mother. These fourteen pastors had all been involved in his mother's and father's lives at one time or another.

> AS PARENTS, CHURCHES, AND A SOCIETY, WE SEEM TO HAVE LOST TRACK OF HOW MUCH OUR CHILDREN RESPOND TO WHAT WE VALUE.

The pastor said the entire family was there. When I asked him what he meant by "the entire family," he stated that his parents had twenty-one children, seventeen of whom were still living. At that time there were forty-three grandchildren and fifty-one great-grandchildren. He then made a casual statement that nearly knocked me out of my chair: "You know, the funny part is that we're all in ministry."

I looked at him for a moment and asked, "Do you mean the children?"

"No, not just my brothers and sisters and me. All of us."

"You mean the grandchildren?"

"Yes." And before I could respond, he added, "And the great-grandchildren, too!"

This family numbered 111 plus spouses: 17 children, 43 grandchildren, and 51 great-grandchildren. All 111 and their spouses came together to celebrate the life and death of his mother. Families just don't gather like that anymore—even for funerals. As shocking as that was, I couldn't get over the fact that they were all in ministry.

I asked him to clarify: "Every single one of them?"

"Absolutely," he exclaimed. "From pastors to missionaries to lay leaders to evangelists. And many of the younger children are already involved with their parents."

## A Father's Legacy

I asked the pastor if he could explain this. He paused for a moment and then spoke as nonchalantly as if he were ordering a pizza. "I guess it's because my father placed such a high value on those in ministry that we all wanted to be a part of what Dad valued so much."

"Was your dad in ministry?" I asked.

"Oh no, my parents were vegetable farmers. I can remember that when I was child, my dad would gather the vegetables into a horse-drawn wagon to take them to the market every week. Before he left, he filled a number of small paper bags with vegetables. My father knew exactly how many pastors and their families lived on the route he traveled to take the vegetables to market. As he traveled to the market every week, he would stop and place a bag of vegetables at every pastor's door."

I shook my head in amazement. Seeing my reaction, he said, "My father would then buy fruit for our family, and he would also buy enough fruit to fill the same number of paper bags—because he would then drop off a bag of fruit at each pastor's house on the way home. I cannot remember a week, regardless of the weather or even how poor the crop, that my father didn't embark upon this routine—until he was unable to travel any longer. Our dad didn't have to tell us he valued pastors; we saw it. And to this day it is his legacy that runs through our family."

> "YOU KNOW, THE FUNNY PART IS THAT WE'RE ALL IN MINISTRY."

Although his father had died many years before his mother, the legacy was indelibly engraved in the family. One hundred eleven family members and their spouses are all serving the Lord because one vegetable farmer let his life truly show what he valued.

## Expect the Best

To see what is of value, parents must look with God's eyes. We must align our actions with our words regarding what we say we value. And as we look at our children through God's eyes to see their true value, we must learn to *expect the best.*

If there is one thing I could change about my past as a father, it would be that I would always expect the best of and for my children. Don't confuse that with demanding perfection or even demanding a certain level of performance. Give them a chance. If we want to raise our kids to keep the faith, I suggest that the formula is far simpler than we have made it. Make every effort to see them with God's eyes, bless them into their future and destiny, and *expect the best*. After all, they are *God's best!*

## FOR PERSONAL REFLECTION OR GROUP DISCUSSION

1. What would the things in your life indicate that you value the most?

2. How well do the things in your life that you *actually* value match what you *say* is important?

3. In our society, why is it so difficult to expect the best for our children?

4. What legacy do you honestly believe will be passed on to your children's children?

5. Is there anything more important than raising your kids to keep their faith?

# APPENDIX A

# ADDITIONAL READING

Barna, George. *Real Teens: A Contemporary Snapshot of Youth Culture.* Ventura, Calif.: Regal, 2001.

———. *Baby Busters: The Disillusioned Generation.* Chicago: Northfield, 1992.

———. *Generation Next: What You Need to Know About Today's Youth.* Ventura, Calif.: Regal, 1995.

Beausay, William, II. *Boys: Shaping Ordinary Boys Into Extraordinary Men.* Nashville: Nelson, 1994.

Bolden, Tonya, ed. *Rites of Passage.* New York: Hyperion, 1994.

Bourne, Jr., Lyle E., and Bruce R. Ekstrand. *Psychology.* 3rd ed. New York: Holt, Rinehart and Winston, 1979.

Brodsky, Jeff. *Stepping Into Adulthood: Discovering the Most Significant Event in Your Child's Life.* Phoenix: ACW Press, 1997.

Bundschuh, Rick. *Passed Thru Fire: A Call for a Christian Rite of Passage to Guide Boys into Godly Manhood.* Wheaton, Ill.: Tyndale, 2003.

Burns, Jim. *Surviving Adolescence.* Ventura, Calif.: Regal, 1997.

Burton, Jim. *Legacy Builders.* Memphis: Brotherhood Commission, SBC, 1996.

Canfield, Ken, Ph.D. *The Heart of a Father.* Chicago: Northfield, 1996.

Coleman, James William, and Donald R. Cressey. *Social Problems.* 4th ed. Grand Rapids, Mich.: Harper & Row, 1990.

Dalbey, Gordon. *Father and Son: The Wound, the Healing, the Call to Manhood.* Nashville: Nelson, 1992.

DeVries, Mark. *Family-Based Youth Ministry.* Downers Grove, Ill.: InterVarsity Press, 1994.

Dobson, James. *Preparing for Adolescence.* Ventura, Calif.: Regal, 1999.

Downs, Perry G. *Teaching for Spiritual Growth: An Introduction to Christian Education.* Grand Rapids, Mich.: Zondervan, 1994.

Dryfoos, Joy G. *Safe Passage.* New York: Oxford University Press, 1998.

Dworetzky, John P. *Introduction to Child Development.* 3rd ed. New York: West Publishing, 1987.

Dyet, Jim, and Jim Russell. *The Master's Plan for Your Family.* Lansing, Mich.: The Amy Foundation, 2003.

Eldredge, John. *Wild At Heart: Discovering the Secret of a Man's Soul.* Nashville: Nelson, 2001.

Elium, Don, and Jeanne Elium. *Raising a Son: Parents in the Making of a Healthy Man.* Berkeley, Calif.: Celestial Arts, 1996.

_____. *Raising a Daughter: Parents in the Making of a Healthy Woman*. Berkeley, Calif.: Celestial Arts, 1996.

Farris, Michael. *How a Man Prepares His Daughters for Life*. Minneapolis: Bethany, 1996.

Floyd, Ronnie W. *The Meaning of a Man*. Nashville: Broadman & Holman, 1996.

Frost, Jack. *Experiencing the Father's Embrace*. Lake Mary, Fla.: Charisma House, 2002.

Garborg, Rolf. *The Family Blessing: Creating a Spiritual Covering for Your Family's Future*. Lakeland, Fla.: White Stone, 2001.

Gardner, John W. *Excellence: Can We Be Equal and Excellent Too?* New York: Harper & Row, 1961.

Grimes, Ronald L. *Deeply into the Bone: Re-Inventing Rites of Passage*. Berkeley, Calif.: University of California Press, 2000.

Hamrin, Robert. *Great Dads*. Colorado Springs: Cook Communications Ministries, 2002.

Hastings, Wayne. *If You Take My Hand, My Son: Leading a Boy to be a Man of God*. Colorado Springs: Cook Communications Ministries, 2001.

Henslin, Earl R. *Man to Man: Helping Fathers Relate to Sons and Sons Relate to Fathers*. Nashville: Nelson, 1993.

Hill, Craig. *Bar Barakah: A Parent's Guide To a Christian Bar Mitzvah*. Littleton, Colo.: Family Foundations Publishing, 1998.

_____. *The Ancient Paths*. Littleton, Colo.: Family Foundations International, 1992.

Howe, Neil, and William Strauss. *Millennials Rising: The Next Generation*. New York: Vintage, 2000.

Hunt, Susan. *Heirs of the Covenant*. Wheaton, Ill.: Crossway, 1998.

Hutchcraft, Ron. *The Battle for a Generation*. Chicago: Moody, 1996.

Jenson, Ron and Matt. *Fathers and Sons*. Nashville: Broadman & Holman, 1998.

Johnson, Greg, and Mike Yorkey. *Faithful Parents, Faithful Kids*. Wheaton, Ill.: Tyndale, 1993.

_____. *Man in the Making: What You Need to Know As You're Becoming a Man*. Nashville: Broadman & Holman, 1997.

Joy, Donald M. *Becoming a Man: A Celebration of Sexuality, Responsibility, and the Christian Young Man*. Nappanee, Ind.: Evangel, 2001.

_____. *Celebrating the New Woman in the Family*. Anderson, U.K.: Bristol Books, 1994.

_____. *Empower Your Kids to be Adults*. Nappanee, Ind.: Evangel, 2000.

Kesler, Jay, with Ronald A. Beers. *Parents and Teenagers: A Guide to Solving Problems and Building Relationships*. Wheaton, Ill.: Victor, 1984.

Kidder, Virelle. *Loving, Launching and Letting Go*. Nashville: Broadman & Holman, 1995.

Kimmel, Tim. *Why Christian Kids Rebel*. Nashville: W Publishing Group, 2004.

Krieder, Larry. *The Cry for Spiritual Fathers and Mothers*. Ephrata, Wash.: House to House Publications, 2000.

Larson, Bart, and Wendell Amstutz. *Youth Violence and Gangs*. Minnesota: National Counseling Resource Center, 1995.

Lee, Steve, Ed.D., and Chap Clark. *Boys to Men: How Fathers Can Help Build Character in Their Sons*. Chicago: Moody, 1995.

LeLaCheur, Dan. *Generational Legacy*. Eugene, Ore.: Family Survival, Inc., 1994.

_____. *Generational Legacy: Study Guide*. Eugene, Ore.: Family Survival, Inc., 1994.

Lewis, Gary and Merrilee. *Is He a Man or Just Another Guy?* Bend, Ore.: GLO Publishing, 2002.

Ligon, William T., Sr. *Imparting the Blessing*. Brunswick, Maine: The Father's Blessing, 1989.

Lewis, Robert. *Raising a Modern-Day Knight: A Father's Role in Guiding His Son to Authentic Manhood*. Colorado Springs: Focus on the Family, 1997.

Lord, Peter M. *Bless and Be Blessed*. Grand Rapids, Mich.: Revell, 2004.

Long, Jimmy. *Generating Hope: A Strategy for Reaching The Postmodern Generation*. Downers Grove, Ill.: InterVarsity, 1997.

Madden, Myron C. *The Power to Bless*. New Orleans: Insight Press, 1999.

McAllister, Dawson. *Saving the Millennial Generation*. Nashville: Nelson, 1999.

McCartney, Bill. *What Makes A Man?*. Colorado Springs: NavPress, 1992.

McClung, Jr., Floyd. *The Father Heart of God*. Eugene, Ore.: Harvest House, 1985.

McDowell, Josh. *The Disconnected Generation: Saving our Youth from Self-Destruction*. Nashville: W Publishing Group, 2000.

McDowell, Josh, and Bob Hostetler. *Right From Wrong*. Dallas: Word, 1994.

Molitor, Brian D. *A Boy's Passage: Celebrating Your Son's Journey to Maturity*. Colorado Springs: WaterBrook Press, 2001.

Morley, Patrick. *The Young Man in the Mirror: A Rite of Passage into Manhood*. Nashville: Broadman & Holman, 2003.

Morley, Patrick, and David Delk. *The Dad in the Mirror: How to See Your Heart for God Reflected in Your Children*. Grand Rapids, Mich.: Zondervan, 2003.

Oliver, Gary and Carrie. *Raising Sons and Loving It: Helping Your Boys to Become Godly Men*. Grand Rapids, Mich.: Zondervan, 2000.

Papalia, Diane E., Sally Wendkos Olds, and Ruth Duskin Feldman. *Human Development*. 8th ed. New York: McGraw-Hill Higher Education, 2001.

Peel, Bill, and Kathy Peel. *Where is Moses When We Need Him?: Teaching Your Kids the Ten Values that Matter Most*. Nashville: Broadman & Holman, 1995.

Phillips, Ron. *Kisses from the Father*. Tulsa, Okla.: Harrison House, 2003.

Rainer, Thom S. *The Bridger Generation*. Nashville: Broadman & Holman, 1997.

Rice, Wayne. *Cleared for Takeoff*. Nashville: W Publishing Group, 2000.

Rice, Wayne, and David Veerman. *Understanding Your Teenager*. Nashville: W Publishing Group, 1999.

Settersten, Jr., Richard A., Frank F. Furstenberg, Jr., and Ruben C. Rumbaut, eds. *On the Frontier of Adulthood*. Chicago: University of Chicago Press, 2005.

Smalley, Gary, and John Trent. *The Blessing*. New York: Pocket Books, 1986.

_____. *The Hidden Value of a Man*. Colorado Springs: Focus on the Family, 1992.

Smith, Timothy. *The Seven Cries of Today's Teens*. Nashville: Integrity, 2003.

Sommers, Christina Hoff. *The War Against Boys: How Misguided Feminism Is Harming Our Young Men*. New York: Simon & Schuster, 2000.

Steinberg, Laurence. *Adolescence*. 6th ed. New York: McGraw-Hill Higher Education, 2002.

Stringer, Doug. *The Fatherless Generation: Hope for a Generation in Search of Identity*. Shippensburg, Penn.: Destiny Image, 1997.

Van Gennep, Arnold. *The Rites of Passage*. Chicago: University of Chicago Press, 1960.

Tweedell, Cynthia Benn, ed. *Sociology: A Christian Approach for Changing the World*. Marion, Ind.: Triangle, 1989.

Weber, Stu. *Locking Arms*. Sisters, Ore.: Multnomah, 1995.

Webber, Robert E. *Ancient-Future Evangelism: Making Your Church a Faith-Forming Community*. Grand Rapids, Mich.: Baker, 2003.

_____. *The Younger Evangelicals: Facing the Challenges of the New World*. Grand Rapids, Mich.: Baker, 2002.

White, Joe. *Faith Training: Raising Kids Who Love the Lord*. Colorado Springs: Focus on the Family, 1994.

Wilder, E. James. *Just Between Father & Son: A Weekend Adventure Prepares a Boy for Adolescence*. Downers Grove, Ill.: InterVarsity, 1990.

_____. *The Stages of a Man's Life*. Springfield, Mo.: Quiet Waters Publications, 1999.

Wilkinson, Bruce. *The Prayer of Jabez*. Sisters, Ore.: Multnomah Publishers, 2000.

_____. *The Prayer of Jabez Devotional*. Sisters, Ore.: Multnomah Publishers, 2001.

Zoba, Wendy Murray. *Generation 2K: What Parents and Others Need to Know About the Millenials*. Downers Grove, Ill.: InterVarsity Press, 1999.

# APPENDIX B

# A CHOSEN GENERATION SEMINARS AND MINISTRY RESOURCES

*But you are a chosen generation, a royal priesthood, a holy nation,*
*His own special people, that you may proclaim the praises of Him*
*who called you out of darkness into His marvelous light.*
**1 Peter 2:9 (NKJV)**

## Vision

To see an explosion of dynamic intergenerational churches reproducing among God's people.

## Ministry Purpose

A Chosen Generation is a Christ-centered ministry that exists to equip and train leaders with strategic vision, passion, concepts and resources for intergenerational ministry.

## Mission Statement

The mission of A Chosen Generation is to provide leaders with training, resources and strategies in order to strengthen the intergenerational culture and spiritual continuity of the Church, thus helping each person grow in spiritual maturity, as a reproducing disciple.

# MINISTRIES AND TRAINING OF A CHOSEN GENERATION

## Men of Honor & Women of Virtue
### Rites of Passage Weekend Seminar

A Chosen Generation has a highly trained and qualified faculty across the country to assist churches in conducting a Rites of Passage weekend.

## Anchor Points Seminar
### Creating Strategies for InterGenerational Ministry

Anchor Points is a powerful, 8 hour seminar that begins the process of helping churches and ministries understand the need for and how to develop the strategies and resources for InterGenerational ministry.

## The Power of Rites of Passage

A Chosen Generation conducts training seminars to equip and train church leaders with the necessary tools to lead their own church through a Men of Honor & Women of Virtue, Rites of Passage weekend.

## Life Walking

Creating a culture where all generations are "doing life together" is no small task. The concept of Life Walking includes mentoring, coaching and encouraging. Life Walking is not a program. It is a change of how we do business in the church.

## There is No Baton

Seniors are leaving the church at an alarming rate. Much of their departure may be attributed to a cultural mentality that has told them to "pass the baton." We have confused the "mantle of leadership" with the "baton of engagement." If we are to recapture the intergenerational church, we must recapture and re-engage our seniors.

## Leadership Training

A Chosen Generation conducts training designed to meet the needs of specific churches and ministries.

## Journey Women

Ministry of Journey Women is targeted at helping women of all ages develop healthy environments to engage in authentic relationships that will strengthen each of them for the journey of life.

## Contact Information

A CHOSEN GENERATION
PMB #355
11757 W. Ken Caryl Ave., F
Littleton, Colorado 80127

Tel: 303-948-1112
Fax: 303-948-1114
info@achosengeneration.org
www.achosengeneration.org

# NOTES

**CHAPTER 1**

1. Bruce Wilkinson, *The Prayer of Jabez Devotional* (Sisters, OR: Multnomah Publishers, Inc., 2001), pp. 12–13.

**CHAPTER 2**

1. Paul Recer, "NASA 'Culture' Blamed in Report," *Associated Press*, August 23, 2003.
2. Ibid.
3. Ibid.
4. Ron Howard, director, *Apollo 13*, 1995. Jim Lovell, *Lost Moon: The Perilous Voyage of Apollo 13*. Available from Anthony W. Haukap, June 30, 1995, http://myweb.accessus.net/~090/apollo13.html, p. 36.
5. Ibid., p. 45.

**CHAPTER 3**

1. Thom S. Rainer, *The Bridger Generation* (Nashville: Broadman & Holman Publishers, 1997), p. 163.
2. Ibid., p. 169.
3. Ibid.
4. Josh McDowell, "URGENT Message From Josh McDowell," *Beyond Belief Campaign Letter*, 2003, p. 1.
5. Ibid.
6. Ibid.
7. Ron Hutchcraft, *The Battle for a Generation* (Chicago: Moody Press, 1996), p. 10.

**CHAPTER 4**

1. Jack Valenti, "Movie Ratings: How It All Began," Motion Picture Association of America, http://www.mpaa.org/movieratings/about/content.htm (accessed January 20, 2005).
2. Ibid.
3. "Understanding the TV Ratings," http://www.tvguidelines.org/ratings.asp (accessed January 10, 2005), TV Parental Guidelines, Washington, D.C.
4. Ibid.
5. Lindsey Tanner, "High Exposure to TV Sex Affects Teens," (Chicago: Associated Press, Updated 03:46 AM EDT 9/7/04), Pediatrics: http://www.pediatrics.org.
6. American Academy of Child & Adolescent Psychiatry Task Force on Juvenile Justice Reform, October 2001, "Recommendations for Juvenile Justice Reform," Washington, D.C., p. 16 (www.aacap.org).
7. U.S. Department of Justice, Office of Justice Programs, Bureau of Justice Statistics. *A Mid-Decade Status Report, A Criminal Justice Information Policy Report*, Washington, D.C., p. 15, May 1997, NCJ161255.

8. Laurence Steinberg, "Should Juvenile Offenders Be Tried as Adults? A Developmental Perspective on Changing Legal Policies," paper presented as a part of a Congressional Research Briefing titled "Juvenile Crime: Causes and Consequences," Washington, D.C., January 19, 2000. (Address correspondence to author at the Department of Psychology, Temple University, Philadelphia, PA 19122.)

9. Andy Humbles, "Prosecutors Weigh Merits of Charging Kids as Adults," *Tennessean* (Associated Press, updated 12/20/2002), www.tennessean.com/government/archives/04/01/46287614.shtml, (accessed 1/11/2005).

## CHAPTER 5

1. "Most Americans think people need to be 26 to be considered grown-up: Seven steps toward adulthood take five years, NORC [National Opinion Research Center] survey at University of Chicago finds," May 9, 2003, The University of Chicago News Office, available at http://www-news.uchicago.edu/releases/03/030509.adulthood.shtml.

2. Tom Perry, "Tom Perry Column: Adulthood comes later these days," *Green Bay Press Gazette*, posted May 11, 2003 [online], available from terry@greenbaypressgazette.com; Internet, www.greenbaypressgazette.com.

3. Martha Irvine, "Becoming a Grown-Up," Associated Press, May 10, 2003 [online], available from http://www.knoxnews.com/kns/national/article/0,1406, KNS_350_1951101,00.

4. Ibid.

5. Perry, "Adulthood comes later these days."

6. Ibid.

7. Marilyn Gardner, "The Longer Road to Adulthood," *The Christian Science Monitor*, December 18, 2002 [online], available at http://www.csmonitor.com/2002/1218/p14s01-lifp.htm.

8. Laurence Steinberg, "Theoretical Perspectives on Adolescence—Biological Theories," in *Adolescence*, 6th ed. (New York: McGraw-Hill Higher Education, 2002), p. 11.

9. Ibid., p. 15.

10. Ibid.

11. Jay Kesler with Ronald A. Beers, *Parents and Teenagers: A Guide to Solving Problems and Building Relationships* (Wheaton, IL: Victor Books, 1984), p. 19.

12. Donald M. Joy, *Empower Your Kids to Be Adults* (Nappanee, IN: Evangel Publishing House, 2000), p. 56.

13. Ibid., p. 55.

14. Ibid., p. 63.

15. Laurence Steinberg, *Adolescence*, 6th ed. (New York: McGraw-Hill Higher Education, 2002), p. 11.

16. Lance Morrow, "The Boys and the Bees," *Time*, May 31, 1999, p. 110.

## CHAPTER 6

1. Donald M. Joy, *Empower Your Kids to Be Adults* (Nappanee, IN: Evangel Publishing House, 2000), p. 41.

2. Jeff Brodsky, *Stepping into Adulthood* (Phoenix: ACW Press, 1997), p. 73.

3. Bart Larson and Wendell Amstutz, *Youth Violence and Gangs* (Rochester, MN: National Counseling Resource Center, 1995), p. 42.

4. "Sports Hazing Incidents," ESPN Network (ESPN Internet Ventures, June 3, 2002), http://espn.go.com/otl/hazing/list.html (accessed 1/17/05).

5. Ibid.

6. Robert Davis, "Five binge-drinking deaths 'just the tip of the iceberg,'" *USA Today*, October 7, 2004.

7. "The Delinquents," *CBSNews.com*, July 18, 2001, http://www.cbsnews.com/stories/2000/08/22/60II/main226894.shtml (accessed 4/6/2005).

8. As quoted in *Deeply into the Bone* by Ronald Grimes, p. 91. Produced by the Union of International Associations in Brussels, Belgium, and accessible at www.uia.org/uiapubs/pubency.htm.

## CHAPTER 7

1. Mark DeVries, *Family-Based Youth Ministries* (Downers Grove, IL: InterVarsity Press, 1994), p. 21.

2. Larry Kreider, *The Cry for Spiritual Fathers & Mothers* (Ephrata, PA: House to House Publications, 2000), pp. 19–20.

3. DeVries, p. 24.

4. Ibid.

5. Wayne Rice and David Veerman, *Understanding Your Teenager* (Nashville: W Publishing Group, 1999), pp. 27–28.

## CHAPTER 8

1. Laurence Steinberg, "Social Transition," in *Adolescence*, 6th ed. (New York: McGraw-Hill Higher Education, 2002), p. 105.

2. *Oxford Latin Dictionary* (New York: Oxford University Press, 1983), p. 1511.

## CHAPTER 17

1. Gary Smalley and John Trent, *The Blessing* (New York: Pocket Books, 1986), p. 27.

2. Craig Hill, *The Ancient Paths* (Littleton, CO: Craig S. Hill, 1992), p. 69.

3. Ibid., p. 28.

4. Johannes Pedersen, *Israel, Its Life and Culture* (London: Oxford University Press, 1926), p. 194.

## CHAPTER 18

1. *Merriam-Webster's Collegiate Dictionary*, Eleventh Edition (Merriam-Webster, Incorporated, 2003), p. 710.

## CHAPTER 22

1. John W. Gardner, *Excellence* (New York: Harper & Row, 1961), p. 120.

# GET TO KNOW THE AUTHOR

## Rev. Chuck Stecker, D. Min.
### President and Founder

Rev. Chuck Stecker is the President and Founder of A Chosen Generation. Chuck is an ordained minister of the Gospel with the Evangelical Church Alliance and has earned a Doctorate of Ministry specializing in Christian Leadership. As an Army Lieutenant Colonel, Chuck served in various key leadership and staff positions, including 3 years on the Joint Staff in the Pentagon. Chuck has served the Lord in the local church in various ministry and leadership positions. After his retirement, he served with Promise Keepers for three years as the Regional Director of the South-Central Region. In 1997, Chuck launched a ministry, Mission Capable Men, and then A Chosen Generation in 2000.

Chuck uniquely combines several years of business experience, 23 years of military service and over 15 years of full-time ministry to bring forth a clear strategy to equip, train, empower and release a new generation of leaders. He has a passion to see churches return to truly intergenerational communities and develop the clear pathways that keep young adults actively connected to their churches and see them develop into the leaders that will impact every area of our society.

His clear vision and leadership teachings have impacted churches, schools, the military and businesses all over the country and as well as other nations. He is able to boldly challenge men and women of all ages to develop strong moral character and give them principles that they can apply to their lives to become spiritually mature and responsible adults. Chuck has spoken to audiences across the nation and around the world on various subjects including Strategies for Intergenerational Ministry Developing, Becoming Strategic Leaders, Rites of Passage, Mentoring/Coaching, Ministry to Men as well as Character and Integrity Issues.

In addition to Men of Honor Women of Virtue, Chuck has authored several articles and was a contributing author to *Effective Men's Ministry: The Indispensable Toolkit for Your Church*. Chuck has taught at Denver Seminary and Christ for the Nations Institute.

Chuck and his wife Billie make their home in Littleton, Colorado and are a vital part of their home church, Grace Community Church. They have three grown children and three incredible granddaughters.

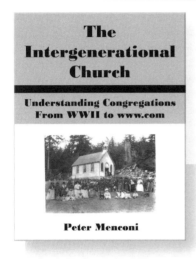

Additional copies of *Men of Honor, Women of Virtue*
and other InterGenerational Resources
are available wherever good books are sold.

If you have enjoyed this book,
or if it has had an impact on your life,
we would like to hear from you.

Please contact us at:

http://seismicpg.com/